To...
Be blessed
Love
Kashina

WHEN
THE SILENCE
SPEAKS

OVERCOMING THE EFFECTS
OF CHILDHOOD SEXUAL ABUSE

KASHINA ALEXANDER-McLEAN

Book Cover Design by HCP Book Publishing

ISBN: 978-1-949343-04-5 (paperback)

TABLE OF CONTENTS

DEDICATION

I wish to dedicate this book to every female who has ever been subjected to any form of sexual abuse, including verbal advances, and has not yet found the courage to speak up about it or the strength to move beyond it.

I want you to know it was never your fault and that you should allow yourself to be angry but also seek the courage and grace to take charge of your life again. Remember, you are beautifully and wonderfully made by God, and even though you may feel cheated on so many levels, please know that God's plan is always to prosper you and not to harm you. All things will work out together for your good if you put your trust in Jesus Christ. I encourage you to be the best you can be and to remind yourself that your circumstances do not make you who you are, but you have the power to create your own circumstances.

I also dedicate this book to everyone who has been a source of strength and a support system to an abuse victim, whether a family member, friend, or acquaintance. Just knowing someone is in our corner can make a lot of difference in our perspective as well as the ability to overcome. Therefore, I want to say, on behalf of every victim, that we appreciate you.

God bless you!

ACKNOWLEDGMENTS

I give thanks first to my Lord and Savior Jesus Christ, who has called, inspired, and equipped me to write this book and positioned me on a path to purpose.

Sincere thanks to my dear husband and Pastor, Reverend Edgar McLean—my strength and motivator—as well as my children for the overwhelming support on this journey.

I also want to say thanks to my friends and prayer partners, Opal and P'Terr-Ann, for constantly covering me in prayer during the times of intense warfare.

To my spiritual fathers and mothers, Pastors Lascelles Bailey and David Grant, Minister Maureen Bailey, and Juliet Grant, as well as my second mother, Mrs. Gauntlett Powell.

To my book coach and publisher, Crystal Daye, who has stood beside me, encouraging me and coaching me through the process.

Last, but not least, to my Esther sisters and everyone else who supported me and contributed to the success of this assignment.

Thank you for being a part of this great accomplishment.

FOREWORD

This is a timely book reminding us of the gracious love of God and His willingness and ability to fix any broken area in our lives. *When the Silence Speaks* is not just a story of childhood sexual abuse and speaking out against it, but it shows in its riveting pages the hand of a mighty God bringing healing and wholeness.

Kashina has aptly described her disappointments with both humans and God, her fears and neglect. She shares in some detail the power of Christ to heal scars and make something beautiful out of what might have been considered ugly and good for nothing.

This book offers hope to those who have and are suffering in silence because of the shame of being sexually abused. It provides the courage to stand up and speak out while offering the soothing balm of forgiveness.

Through her ministry/organization, "Scars that Speak Out Loud," Kashina now takes great delight in empowering the abused to become advocates of change and activists in the proclamation of the gospel of her Lord and Savior Jesus Christ, who has made her whole and is willing to do the same for you.

I encourage you to read and share this awesome, captivating, life-changing book with someone you know who needs to break the silence and be made whole again.

Reverend David Grant

INTRODUCTION

Have you ever been at a point in your life when you felt like everything was stacked against you, and the only way to go is down?

Have you ever felt like you were destined to be unhappy and that God was unfair in allowing all the horrible things to happen to you?

Have you ever asked, "Why me Lord?"

We often struggle to find the answers to the many questions that bombard our minds, and the lack of a possible response tends to only push us deeper into depression.

However, in the midst of my situation, I was met by the presence of a God who knows no limits, who demonstrated such grace and endowed me with the strength and courage to rise above my challenges and be restored.

This life-changing book will demonstrate how these very challenges became the building blocks for reaching my God-given destiny. It will help you find the hope and healing you earnestly desire after living in silence for so long.

This story will give you the courage to triumph over any obstacle you face while providing the comforting relief of forgiveness as you take the first steps to abundant living.

CHAPTER 1

MY CHILDHOOD

"*Just* as He chose us in Him before the foundation of the world, that we should be holy and without blame before Him in love." (Ephesians 1:4).

I was born at the Victoria Jubilee Hospital to Rastafarian parents in the late 70s when Jamaica was terrorized by gangs, drugs, and indescribable violence. Politics and Reggae music were the order of the day and "I feel like bombing a church" was the national anthem in my home. I was indoctrinated into the culture and beliefs of the Rastafarian movement from a very young age and was exposed to marijuana from the womb. My mother had, and still has, a strong Rastafarian background, while my father joined the movement after meeting her, which forced him to be isolated from his side of the family, who did not believe in this lifestyle.

Even though I was born in the city of Kingston, I spent my earlier childhood years in the volatile community of Spanish Town and then eventually moved to rural Jamaica with my immediate family after the gruesome shooting death of one of my father's younger siblings. As children, we learned to play the Congo drum and participated in the various events held by the dreadlocks from both the twelve-tribe group as well as the nyabinghi community. Our lives were typical to that of the lower class Rastas, so it seemed I was automatically destined to be a youngster with fewer opportunities based on the ideals of society at the time.

Following the move to the county, my life could be considered as normal as any little girl my age living in the rural part of

Jamaica in an income restricted household with struggling parents and several mouths to be fed. I was the eldest child of four at the time and the first girl for both parents, who worked hard to ensure that my siblings and I were provided for with the best of what they had. I had two older half-brothers by my father who I barely knew and heard very little about, as it appeared to be a topic that was tabooed in my house. We maintained a very humble lifestyle in a small, underdeveloped community with no access to basic amenities such as roads, electricity, and running water. We were given average exposure to the outside world and were not permitted to visit the neighbour's house or play in the streets like the other kids in my community; instead, we would spend every waking moment reading one book or the other, with the Maccabees Bible being the most popular at the time.

My parents maintained a small backyard garden, and many times this was the source of our daily meals, which mostly consisted of vegetables, peas, and beans as well as ground provisions. There were days when there was absolutely no food at home, so my mother would harvest the red peas from the yard and prepare them with salt for dinner. We would drink the water, eat the peas, and settle for bed satisfied; no one in the community knew what we ate for dinner, as we were not allowed to eat outside the home or ask for assistance. Still, we never complained about not having what we needed, and, if offered food, we politely declined. Life was hard most of the time, and I believe my parents were often overwhelmed with these challenges even though they never expressed any feelings of frustration. Nevertheless, my parents reserved their positions as avid disciplinarians who would ensure that we were always taught to do the right things. They upheld the stance "never save the rod and spoil the child" and, as such, would guarantee a good beating when we failed to live up to the standard they set for our household. My siblings and I were well-mannered children who excelled in both academia as well as extracurricular activities, and I had a fair idea of what I wanted to do with my life from a very young age. I was considered industrious in the home and at school and rarely ever disobeyed those in authority. Though I had an aversion to constantly being reminded by my father that it was four of us and we needed no company, I never went against his instructions, mostly because I was afraid of the beating from my mother. People knew we had lots of potential and always encouraged us when they saw us in the street. The average person in the neighbourhood farmed land, raised animals, and never finished high school, so we were a beacon of light in our little environment. Even though things were hard, we did our best to live up to the expectations of everyone, including my parents, and rarely ever complained.

My mom made school uniforms and school bags for my younger brother and myself out of fabric she purchased at the store in town; the bags served for books as well as the home-cooked vegetarian meals we took to school for lunch. My brother and I endured a lot of stress. We were teased constantly at school, especially when the lunch accidentally spilled on the books and we still had to eat it, but the thought of moving away from this life and making enough money to take care of my family would be my motivation and, as such, I never allowed myself to get discouraged by the teasing. As young as I was, I was driven by the desire to succeed and to help my family. The Rastafarian culture and the extremely austere environment in which we were so aptly brought up also helped to ingrain certain characteristics in us that caused other children, young and old, to admire and emulate us. As a result, the neighbourhood children congregated at our gate and doorstep so we could teach them to read. This exercise, of course, wouldn't be at the top of our list of things to do, as we wanted to play and be like everyone else. We always looked forward to summer, Easter, and Christmas, when we would be off from school and allowed to travel to town to visit and spend time with our grandmother and other family members for the holidays. Apart from holidays, however, things were pretty routine at home. My dad went to work and was only home on weekends, while my mother took care of the house on whatever he provided. She was fierce, and all of us were terrified of her. Sometimes, as children, we preferred to do other things than reading, but we would not consider mentioning it in her hearing. As girls, we were not allowed to wear a perm or jewelry or play with dolls, as this was unacceptable in our home. Disgruntled by some of the rigid rules and regulations at home, I sometimes sat before the piece of broken glass that served as a mirror and argued with my parents behind their backs, but the moment

I felt even the shadow of my mother, I catapulted off the old hassock and found something "constructive" to do. Unlike being at home in the country, there was so much more to do at grandma's, as our uncles and cousins would take us out in the streets and teach us to ride bicycles and scooters as well as drive around town on small errands in old cars. This also gave our parents a break from the everyday task of caring for us, allowing for some time to rest.

As the day drew closer once again for the much-anticipated holiday adventure, we discussed the different things we would do and imagined the looks on the faces of our relatives when we arrived in the family yard. Nothing else seemed to matter during these last few days, as all we could think and talk about was our trip. The night before the trip was usually the longest night ever, and as our custom was every holiday, we would sit in a row at the top of the prickly old spring-filled double bed that the four of us shared, with our feet nicely tucked under the old spread. We were so excited for morning that we usually could not sleep that night. My siblings and I watched and waited anxiously as the morning sun snuck its way into existence, and the moment we could feel the warmth of the rays on our happy little faces, we would be out of bed and ready to go. Of course, we had to wait for our parents to wake up, deflate their air bed that would be folded and nicely tucked in a corner after each night's use, and go around in circles doing much of nothing, a routine that seemed to last for ages, and let's not forget the infamous breakfast that was prepared most mornings, which consisted of one serving of aloe blended with freshly juiced orange and egg white that was supposed to "clean us out," a cup of cerasee tea, and a bowl of cornmeal porridge with coconut milk.

It was finally time to depart, and we were all bursting with excitement. The four of us made our way to the old ford escort that had more colours than the rainbow, and after several moments of fighting about who would sit at the good window and being shouted at a few times by our mother, with some expletives being uttered, the long-anticipated journey began. A journey that, under normal circumstances, should take about three and a half hours, took a lot longer as the car struggled through Fern Gully, up Mount Rosser, across the flat bridge, with episodes of shutting off and even more episodes of overheating, and everyone coming out to help push. After several hours, we finally made it to our destination, and even the animals seemed excited to see us. Everyone was delighted, including the folks who convinced themselves they were our relatives because they would linger at my grandma's front step for dinner each evening.

Being at this place once again was like a dream come true. The black mangoes had begun to ripen, and one could smell the sweet aroma in the air, all the trees were now laden with fruit, grandma's tasty fried sprat and bread were also ready and waiting, and the loud chatter from everyone filled the atmosphere. It seems life could not have been better even for a few weeks, and my mission was to enjoy it to the fullest before going back home to my regular routine of being the perfect child.

It was now early evening, and our other family members were present by now. As we did each year, we met a few new ones too, and this only made the adventure more exhilarating. This is what we had been waiting for, freedom, freedom to play in the streets, freedom to not have to take up a book, freedom to just be kids. By this time, everyone had eaten their fill and exchanged a few greetings and courtesies, our parents had now left for the country, and the fun was set to begin with the traditional story time—first by our great-grandmother, who spoke about when she was young over seventy years ago and then by the extended family, as everyone had something to share. We all sat under the big mango tree sharing and listening to these different stories, which ranged from life experiences to fiction and the untameable imagination of people who had nothing to share but wanted to compete to see who could tell the scariest tale. Then it was time to set out for the outside toilet in the middle of the night, and we would all be afraid and had to depend on grandma to accompany us.

Grandma was always said to be one of the prettiest, most sought-after women in her community. She was short in stature and of a cool, dark complexion. She had extremely long, soft, curly hair that would flow behind her tiny frame as she walked, while the unruly ones at the front danced frivolously in the wind, complementing her dark, cool skin that everyone admired over the years. She was fun to be around and was like the more relaxed version of my mother. Despite the obvious wrinkles, her eyes sparkled just the same, and the partially white dentures were also still breath-taking. Her hair was now mostly grey at the roots, revealing the many years they had seen, but she still loved to reminisce on the many beauty pageants she used to win in her community back in her day. It was a pleasure to sit and listen to her as she traveled back in time down memory lane, giving us a tiny glimpse of what life was like in the forties and fifties. She has experienced a tremendous amount of hardship throughout the years, which includes having to raise her eight children by herself while doing odd jobs, as well as the death of three of her boys, and it was beginning to tell its tale on her face. But though she looked as if she was getting tired day by day, she was always available to anyone who passed by her rackety old shop and shouted out to her in that bellowing tone. She was loved by everyone, and one could understand why, as she was an outgoing, seemingly selfless person who enjoyed serving the people in her community and being a mother to those she didn't give birth to. She was a strong, determined, independent woman; a Warrior Princess in my eyes, who worked very hard every day tending to her multitude of animals, caring for her now mostly adult children while operating a small shop from her front yard that fed the whole community. She smiled a lot, was friendly, and rarely ever said no. This caused her to become extremely exhausted by the end of each day, and with a cigarette hanging in the corner of her mouth, she often nodded off to sleep in the evenings while sitting in the veranda chair as if she was in malice with her bed, a bed that would probably serve three or more people for the night anyway.

She worked hard all her life to build a home for her family, and even in her old age; she still felt the need to work hard to maintain what she considered her legacy. Her boys always got themselves in trouble, so she had to find ways to rescue them from the consequences that followed their careless, inconsiderate actions. Many of her later years were spent at the police station trying to negotiate their release, and as soon as they saw the light of day, they reverted to their old ways, causing her much pain and heartache. She never complained as she felt it was her motherly responsibility and often said, "They are mine already."

I frequently thought she was too easy on them, but the unspoken rule that a child must not speak to an adult in that way prevented me from expressing my opinion. Nevertheless, from time to time, I felt sorry for her and wished she would stop breastfeeding these big men who I felt needed to take responsibility for themselves and their actions.

CHAPTER 2

MY FIRST ENCOUNTER

It was another highly anticipated summer holiday, very much like all the others, and, like my siblings, I too looked forward to visiting my family in town. The level of excitement was just as high as it was the first day we went back to visit them after moving to the country, and the course of events pretty much took place in the same order as always, except this time around I was about to experience something I never anticipated. My life, as I knew it, was about to change for the worst, but I had no clue of what was about to take place.

We had just finished our traditional storytelling while eating fish and bread and barely settled off to bed in the not so early hours of the night when it first happened. I was sleeping beside my Warrior Princess (Grandma) on the front end of the bed, while she slept at the inside corner. At first, it felt like a nightmare. Everyone else was asleep by now, and as I laid there beside her half asleep, the last moment of my innocent childhood was violently taken away from me by people who had the responsibility to protect me. Initially, it felt like a huge dark mass overshadowed me, and in a matter of minutes, I was pinned helplessly to the bed, unable to take a good breath. I was very frightened and unsure about what was ensuing, but as I tried to move, I suddenly realized that I was trapped under this person's weight. A million thoughts immediately raced through my mind as I tried to determine what was going on. Unable to come to a rational conclusion, I narrowed it down to the fact that it must have been one of the ghosts from the stories they told us. He whispered something in my ear, and, though inaudible, it sounded terrifying to me.

I tried to scream, I tried to move, I tried to reach out and touch my Warrior Princess. I shuddered in fright, but he quickly covered my mouth with his large, hard, dirty hands that smelled like old car wheels, preventing me from making the slightest sound. I could taste his salty sweat on my tongue as I struggled relentlessly to escape the grips of what seemed like hell, and suddenly a nauseating feeling came over me as I wrestled hopelessly between breathing, screaming, and dying. I tried desperately with everything in me to fight, but, of course, I was no contest for this almost six feet male figure on top of me. As he effortlessly overpowered his prey, I could feel the cold walls becoming one with my tiny frame. I frantically attempted to reach beside me again for Warrior Princess, but she was fast asleep and totally oblivious to what was going on next to her. The dreadful physical pain of this mortifying experience, which felt like hours and hours of unending torture, as well as the awful feeling of fear, ripped through my frail eight-year-old body with every disgusting stroke. I felt as if all my blood vessels collapsed inside of me at once, and I convinced myself that anything would be better than this, even death. While the tears gently caressed my colourless cheeks in forced silence, and my body trembled in terror, afraid to wake up my other family members in the small two-bedroom house, I clenched my teeth as hard as I could and closed my eyes so tight I saw flashing lights. I felt battered, alone, angry, confused, terrified, severely scarred, and powerless. After what seemed to be a long while, I noticed I didn't feel the aggressive movement inside of me anymore, but the excruciating pain was still very much intense. I soon realized he was finished and could feel when the weight of his oversized body lifted from off me. He pulled my clothing in place, tucked me in bed nicely, and kissed me on the forehead before exiting the room, leaving me in a deep pit of despair, a pool of blood, and a world of complete silence and darkness. Warrior Princess was so tired that night she never woke up, she never moved a muscle, she could not rescue me from the monster that she knew too well, or so I thought.

I lay in that bed completely paralyzed with pain for the rest of the night, trying to make sense in my mind of what had just taken place, but, of course, I could not even fathom it. I was shaking in horror and was so afraid to even open my eyes, though I couldn't go back to sleep. The morning seemed to take a long time to make its appearance this time around, and the wait became increasingly unbearable as the hours slowly crept by. I began to cry aloud and then quietly, as I had absolutely no idea what else to do. I was not only mystified, but I was badly hurt, to the point where I could not move, but Warrior Princess still wouldn't wake up. I became aware of the frightening reality of how badly I was bleeding, and now more than ever, sleep evaded me for the rest of the night. Even when it was day, it still felt dark and heavy in this new world that was created for me. I wanted to say something to someone, but how could I tell? I couldn't. I was so scared, I didn't know what else to do but cry. No one paid any attention to the fact that I was evidently traumatized, no one noticed that the playful, bubbly child that was present just yesterday had suddenly disappeared, no one noticed that I was gone. I was assisted to get out of bed before the break of day and went outside with Warrior Princess, who helped me to shower and returned to bed before everyone else was awoken. I don't know what happened to the clothes I was wearing that night, but I do not recall seeing them again since. As the other kids got up to their usual routine, I stayed inside broken, listening to the outbursts of laughter, and watching them through the glass window as they frolicked in the busy yard. I didn't want to play that day, as I was still in a lot of pain, I was overwhelmed with fear, and I felt sick to my stomach. My siblings and my younger family members made several failed attempts to encourage me to come out and play, but I refused and simply told them I was feeling sick. I really didn't feel I could stand being outside anyway. I didn't want anyone to see me, I wanted to hide for as long as I could, as far away as I could, but where would I go so no one would find me? I was hungry and thirsty but had absolutely no appetite for food, as all the while I laid there I was worried that the ghost would return to haunt me again that night. Just as I feared, my worst nightmare repeated itself in its most gruesome form.

As I did the night before, I went to bed just like everyone else did, except I couldn't sleep this time. I saw when he stealthily approached the bedside, and though I wanted to scream, I couldn't; instead, I froze. He was my favorite of all the others, as even though he was about ten years my senior, he was still the youngest of them all. We related well with him, especially during the fun story times. I never understood why he would do this to me, and with the question signs in my eyes, I stared at him in complete astonishment. In silence, I begged him not to proceed by constantly shaking my head, but he refused to pay attention to my nonverbal cue and instead placed his index finger over his lips signaling to me to be quiet. It felt even more horrible than it did before, maybe because I was anticipating it and was already severely bruised inside, riddled with fear of the thought that it was really happening again. I began to cry even before he touched me. I cringed and clung unto thin air failing to catch a single breath and refusing to allow myself to feel during each gut-wrenching experience as he aggressively reduced me to a worthless piece of nothing in his hands. Little did I know that the worst was still yet to come, little did I know that there were others waiting to partake. I thought he must have invited these two other relatives, who were older than himself, to join him. I assumed he told them about it. He must have told them exactly where to come and what to do because they seemed to know the routine so well as if they had been there before. And night after night after night they would all come, they would all aggressively take, they would all hurt me. One, then two, then three of them would come. It's such a pity Warrior Princess was always so tired that she could never wake up to help me; there was no one to help me.

For the duration of the summer holiday, the nightmares began to grow in frequency and intensity after that first night, as the three of them took turns each night to mutilate my smaller than average body, leaving me in total anguish and misery.

For the first time, I wanted so badly to go back home because I was in constant pain, but my mother and father were nowhere near; family members had turned into evil people who I felt I barely knew, and Warrior Princess was always too tired to help me escape. The wonderful highly anticipated summer holiday that should have been filled with fun had turned into a most horrifying, gruesome, frightening experience for an innocent eight-year-old girl who would never know sweet sleep again. Yet, every holiday after that, my siblings and I were shipped off by my parents to grandma's house again and again, and every night of every holiday, I endured the pain and dread of being sexually abused by several of my family members. I was destroyed, in more ways and in more places than I will ever be able to explain fully with just words. I felt as if they went way down inside me, inside my soul, with each sordid encounter and compelled it to gradually pass away, while I watched helplessly. My body wasn't even mine anymore. It felt as if it solely belonged to them, since they did with it as they pleased, whenever they wanted to, without any thought or feeling of how it may have affected me. Everything I was and all I wanted to be was now open to the mercy of these immoral elements and was ripped away from me, leaving me with no other option but to sit in silence and wait, hoping it would all disappear, that I would somehow forget and stop hurting. I barely understood that the hurt was just beginning because, at eight years old, it was difficult to identify with what I was feeling. This was simply the beginning of the rest of my life, which became a very difficult process, to say the least. This was the foundation of all the ill decisions and events that ultimately became the building blocks to the life of a troubled girl who everyone later decided would never amount to anything. This was the source of the loud silence that blared in my head every day since that summer holiday. This was the reason for all the anger, the hate, the guilt, and the shame I walked around with constantly for many years, wearing it like a badge of honour on my shoulders. This was the source of the thwarted image I had of myself, emotionally disfigured, spiritually debilitated, and psychologically flawed. This was the reason for giving up on my dreams, going after the things that would only harm me. This was the reason I self-destructed. Being raped as an innocent child, especially by people you love and trust, is one of the most traumatizing experiences you could ever possibly have. It is difficult to fully explain how it made me feel, except to say that I was murdered. I was alive, but I couldn't live anymore. I repressed the thoughts and feelings and tried as best as I could to live a "normal" childhood and even adulthood for many years, even though the abuse continued way into my older teenage years. I know my story is not unique to me, and I am sharing it, so others will know they are not alone and there is hope.

Whether you are a child, a relative, or a parent, you would have heard at some point in your life about children being molested and raped by their family members, family friends, trusted adults, or even total strangers. You may be tempted to believe this will never happen to you or your family; you may feel secure in your environment just like I did before everything went wrong. Let me encourage you parents to be aware of what is happening in the lives of your children, as this can mean the difference between their physical and emotional health and well-being or the lack thereof. Let me encourage you to make yourself aware of the signs of sexual abuse in children, which includes, but are not limited to, nightmares, becoming withdrawn or secretive, fear, anger, acting out, or self-harm. These are just some of the issues I faced during and after my ordeal. Listen to your children and teach them as early as they can understand to say no to anything and anyone who makes them uncomfortable in any way as well as to report it to you. No one is immune, so be aware, be alert, and be educated.

CHAPTER 3

A SHIFT IN PERSPECTIVE

After every ordeal, I would go home to my family, but no one knew what had taken place while I was away. I didn't say anything to anyone; I didn't feel I could. I was afraid of what would happen if I did, so I kept it a secret from my family. I never wanted to go back to grandma's house, and even though I asked my parents to let me stay home with them, I could not give them a valid reason to oblige. My mother would get upset every time I mentioned it, my father would end up arguing with her for getting mad at me for nothing, and the home environment that was once quiet and peaceful had now become scary and unhappy. I soon realized I was the reason for the constant arguments, so I decided to never ask again to stay home for holidays.

As the years progressed, Easter, summer, and Christmas would never be the same again. Every year, three times per year, my younger siblings and I would be taken to grandma for the holidays. And every year, I would relive the nightmares night after night, with no one to rescue me from these evil men. I gradually forced myself into a place of inconsolable despondency and became like a piece of log; a cold, lifeless piece of log, with no feeling at all. My nights felt as if they lasted longer than usual. After they were done gratifying themselves, I would lie in bed staring at the old zinc roof, crying uncontrollably, wishing myself away, but nothing happened. The more I wished, the more it hurt, and the more the tears came in silence. In the mornings, I tried to wash away the feeling, the hurt, and the shame by taking long showers under the big standpipe in the old outside bathroom, but while the showers became longer, the pain became more intense.

Scared to death and in constant anguish, I compelled myself to wander to a time when I would be like the other children, eating mangoes, fish, and bread, listening to stories, and playing in the yard. I knew it was real, but I pretended it wasn't, trying to convince myself that it would go away, and that tomorrow would be better, but tomorrow never came. Tomorrow got lost in the darkness of today, and night after night, when everyone else was asleep, my body became someone else's. There was nothing I could do but cry, while the three adult men took turns satisfying their immoral, unhealthy appetite one at a time. During the daytime, they would walk by me in the yard to and fro, watching with ravenous eyes, anxiously anticipating nightfall so they could devour my body like starving vultures and rip my soul apart like the ghosts they were. I prayed every day that nightfall wouldn't come, but God never seemed to hear my prayers; maybe He was too busy doing more important things, but then again, I wasn't sure of who He was or whether He knew I even existed. I wasn't sure who to ask for when I called, as I was forbidden to say His name at home; I just wasn't sure.

Every day was spent in fear; I was afraid they would come back, I was afraid they would hurt me if I told, I was afraid my parents and the rest of the family would blame me, I was afraid of the pain, I was afraid of everything and everyone around me. Every night, my heart would be filled with hurt and terror. My eyes became sore from constant crying, and I longed to see my mother; as fierce as she was, I would prefer to be in her presence, but that day wouldn't come for another few weeks. I had to endure the suffering until it was time to return home after the holiday season. Maybe the little "tokens of love" left under my pillow each night should have made it better over time. Although I had no idea who left it there, I knew it belonged to me, but that didn't help; it only made me feel worse inside. I began to hate myself and those who were given the responsibility to protect and care for me, but no one noticed that I was becoming angry as the nightmares continued for many years to come.

The physical pain became more bearable as the years progressed and I mastered the art of traveling back and forth in my mind to my safe place, where I would become the log and not feel anything, except hate and anger toward everyone around me, including myself. I had now learned the art and science of pretending to be okay and convinced myself and, sometimes, believed that I was fine. I wanted to hurt my relatives, and I wanted to hurt myself even more. I developed an intense level of anger toward my mother in particular, as I thought she was insensitive and uncaring. She would often tell me I was a pig because I sometimes snapped at my younger siblings, who often got on my nerves. Never did I feel she took the time to find out why I became so aggressive. There were so many scars that even I did not understand; deep wounds I never even knew existed. I blamed myself, as I was a little over eleven by now, and I should know better than to let them continue to hurt me. Why didn't I stop them? Why did I allow them to carry on with absolutely no consequence for their actions? I knew it was wrong, but I was scared to death of what would happen if I told. At other times, I thought maybe if no one knew, it would be better for everyone. What would my friends at school, siblings, and cousins think? What would my parents say if they knew? Maybe my mother would beat me, as most things were usually my fault given that I was the eldest child. I was mystified and distraught, wanting to run away but scared to even do that. I created a world for myself in the midst of all that was happening. I knew it wasn't real, but it was the only place I felt safe.

My grandmother became a stranger in my eyes, and I was no longer mesmerized by the thought of her when she was younger; I no longer felt safe at her home, I no longer enjoyed her fried sprat and bread that she would prepare in anticipation of our visit. I no longer saw her as the great Warrior Princess; I no longer thought she was caring and beautiful. Everything and everyone was ugly. My grades fell at school, and after a while, my teacher noticed that I was not only getting into more fights every day but was becoming angrier and more withdrawn. She didn't punish me but simply instructed me to change my seat to one at the front of the class just so she could keep an eye on me, and I could stay out of trouble. I grew even more distant from the children at school because they teased me every day because I often wet myself on the way to the washroom. I was embarrassed to be at school, I didn't like being at home, and I was afraid to be at grandmas. I felt alone and began to avoid the playground, eating my homemade lunch at the back of the school or sitting alone in class while everyone else went out to play. The drive and desire I had to succeed slowly dissipated. All I could think of, despite how hard I tried not to, or how I told myself I was fine, was the night when the nightmares took place. When I tried to sleep at nights, I had flashbacks of the events and cried in my bed while my other siblings slept. I did not like them either, as they seemed to be living a normal life, free from the pain I was forced to endure. I hated God because, whether I knew His name or not, I expected He would protect me from these evil people, but, instead, He sat in His lofty chair and allowed them to hurt me over and over.

Where was all the discipline my parents tried to instill in us when we were younger? I was no longer the well-mannered student, and although I had a fair idea of what I wanted to do with my life, it didn't seem to matter at this point. I no longer cared whether I was seen as the industrious girl at home, and I rarely listened to those who were in authority anymore. Living up to everyone's expectations was the least important thing to me. I felt cheated and betrayed.

My teacher, at the time, seemed to know something was awfully wrong with me, and she attempted to communicate with me more often. I still could not disclose the real issue, but her concern was a slight glimmer of hope that the world wasn't all it seemed to be. It was as if the no-name God really did hear my prayers after all and answered them in His own way, as He sent me someone who would make me feel like more than just a log. She didn't know about the nightmares, yet she demonstrated a great level of concern for my well-being and was consistent in her efforts to make sure I was okay. I spoke to her about other things unrelated to the events, and she encouraged me to pursue my dreams at all cost. She was the only person who knew I wanted to become a nurse because we spent every break period together talking about what I wanted to become when I grew up, which school I wanted to attend after my common entrance exam, and how I was going to live far away from home. She helped me to re-focus on things that were once important to me and ensured I studied real hard for the exam, so I could attend my school of choice. I heeded every word that came from her mouth. That became the only thing I felt I could do for myself, and I was determined to do it as best as I could.

The results finally came in, and I passed my exam with a decent enough grade on the first attempt, thanks to my teacher. I was the first person in the history of my family to pass the common entrance up to that point and move on to high school. Everyone was proud of me, and my family showered me with small gifts. For a moment, I felt normal; for one moment, I gave no thought to the nightmares or those who caused them; for a moment, I forgot that it would be summer in a few weeks, but only for a moment.

"This mean you is a big girl now," one relative whispered as he secretly expressed his desire for me, growing more intense.

I ignored his unsolicited comment and tried to continue to enjoy the compliments and positive feedback I was receiving from the rest of the family, but that awful statement kept ringing in my ears like a blaring siren, and a new measure of hatred began to grow instantaneously.

The remaining summer holiday continued as usual with the nightmares each night, while my parents were back at home preparing what they could for the new school year, totally oblivious to what was taking place. It was time for high school now, and I wasn't sure what to expect or how I would fit in. I wasn't sure if I could hide the scars in my soul, but I knew I was looking forward to my first day at my new school. I was a bit disappointed, as I was not placed in my school of choice, but, nevertheless, I was not perturbed by it for too long. I was excited about high school, and that's all that mattered at the time. Initially, it didn't seem to be a challenge, as I did well for the first two years or so. My siblings and I still went to town every year during the holidays. The nightmares continued every night, except they weren't so scary anymore since I could separate my thoughts from what my body was going through. There were also several young men who would hang around grandma's that I had become close to, and they would talk to me now as if I was their age. I enjoyed their company because I could no longer relate to my happy, playful cousins and siblings. I spent a lot of time talking with these guys about so many things, not realizing that the enemy was setting me up once again. After a while, I forgot about the talks I used to have with my teacher. I began to stay outside during class time to hang out with my new friends, who were also mostly male, and sell the marijuana I stole from my parents. I only cared that the money was coming in and that I would have enough to gamble at the end of the day. For the first time in a long time, I felt a sense of being in control, and the beatings from my mom, though inevitable, were not such a great concern for me at this point. I told myself I had felt worst pain in my life; at least this pain wouldn't hurt so deep. The grades were beginning to fall again, but in my youthful exuberance and determination to please myself, I gave no attention to that and never thought about the consequences.

The warm sun rays danced on my face through the clear windscreen as we drove through Fern Gully yet another time while I watched the tall fern trees overlapping to create a blanket to hide the asphalt from the strength of the morning sun. We were on our way to grandmas for the holidays again, but this time would be different. I was no longer the happy, unsuspecting little eight-year-old girl; I was determined to do whatever I had to do to defend myself. *Enough is enough!* I thought, as the screaming silence in my mind drove me into a frenzy. I stopped as I remembered that I was not alone and quietly planned how I would handle the situation this time around. My siblings were their usual enthusiastic self, totally unaware of the volcano erupting inside of me, and my parents, well, they were just there, as usual.

My plan was perfect; after this, they would know they should not mess with me; they would never be able to touch me again because I was going to make the whole world know what was taking place all this time. I was going to stand up to each of them when they came to me like they usually did. I was going to fight back. One of my three deranged family members met us at the entrance of the yard with his usual gleeful grin. He had two fewer teeth than he did the last time I saw him and looked even more like a raggedy old bum. I figured the liquor had begun to set in by now, as it was around midday and well into his regular daily routine of drinking, smoking, and loud, nonsensical, boisterous chatter with men of like mind, who convinced themselves that they were actually making sense. I hurriedly made my way out of the car to put my bags away, all the while thinking of how I would execute my plan when the need arose. But as soon as he came closer and asked for a hug, I froze, completely dismissed the thought of my mission, and the cycle continued. I felt like a prisoner in my own skin; wanting to escape to freedom but trapped behind the walls of fear. I felt like the Psalmist when he wrote the following prayer in Psalm 57:

> *Be merciful to me, O God, be merciful to me! For my soul trusts in You; and in the shadow of Your wings I will make my refuge, until these calamities have passed by. I will cry out to God Most High, to God who performs all things for me. He shall send from heaven and save me; He reproaches the one who would swallow me up. Selah.*

God shall send forth His mercy and His truth. My soul is among lions; I lie among the sons of men who are set on fire, whose teeth are spears and arrows, and their tongue a sharp sword. Be exalted, O God, above the heavens; let Your glory be above all the earth. They have prepared a net for my steps; my soul is bowed down; they have dug a pit before me; into the midst of it they themselves have fallen. Selah. My heart is steadfast, O God, my heart is steadfast; I will sing and give praise. Awake, my glory! Awake, lute and harp! I will awaken the dawn. I will praise You, O Lord, among the peoples; I will sing to You among the nations. For Your mercy reaches unto the heavens, and Your truth unto the clouds. Be exalted, O God, above the heavens; let Your glory be above all the earth.

I was more than disappointed at my spinelessness, and I knew I needed to be rescued, but, unlike the Psalmist, I never prayed again to the no-name God to deliver me from these evil people because He never seemed to answer me when I did. Instead, I remained in the cycle of pain and terror and hid myself in the guilt and shame of it all.

CHAPTER 4

WHO AM I NOW?

The group I was hanging out with at school was becoming larger by the week, while the income generated from marijuana sales became less. I was smoking marijuana a lot by now, and there was more smoking than selling. In addition to that, the revenue was mainly used to purchase alcohol, as this was found to be a more effective way to forget the nightmares and remain composed. By age sixteen, I was consuming more than two liters of white rum and smoking innumerable joints of marijuana or cigarettes per day while at school instead of going to classes. I was suspended from school for days at a time because of my tardiness and constant involvements in fights but still left the house and loitered on the school campus so my mother would not find out. One adult friend after another would show up as my guardian, and after the suspension period, I would be on my best behavior for the first several weeks or so to avoid being called out at school again. But, eventually, I would return to my normal routine. It was still very difficult at home financially, but never had I thought for a moment to use the money I made to assist with food or any other necessity. Instead, it was solely used to satisfy my appetite for drugs, alcohol, and gambling. As time passed, I began to stay out later and later after school with little fear of the consequences when I got home, and every day I would make my way to the avenue where I engaged in hours of heated winning and losing and winning, though I rarely ever lost. I had fallen into the status quo of the high school I was attending, the family I belonged to, and the community in which I lived. They said that high school did not produce anything good and had warned my mother not to send me there from the beginning. My family had a history of non-progressiveness, and my community, well; it left much to be desired. Once again, I became complacent, with no drive and no desire to succeed at anything.

I also became sexually involved with a few of the young men who would frequent my grandma's house to satisfy something in me that I could not control or understand. It was a bit different with them since I wasn't forced to do anything I didn't want to do. I never dared allow my disturbed abusers who had intensified surveillance on me every moment of the day to see me talking to them, so I would sneak out of the house and meet them at various times at night when everyone else was asleep. This was my version of fun now, and once again, I looked forward to going to town for the holidays, as I would continue to meet the guys for our late-night rendezvous. The abusers were still a part of the big picture, and though very insignificant in my mind by now, I continued to be the instrument of pleasure for three giant men with poor hygiene and alcohol on their breaths. Nevertheless, I was having fun in my own way, with little concern for what anyone would say or think and very little understanding of the repercussions it would have on me both physically, emotionally, and spiritually. I really wanted to stop being my family members' tool but wasn't sure how I would accomplish that. I contemplated in the quiet of my mind many times how I would cease those nightmares but could never find the answer to my question. Not for one moment did it occur to me that maybe my two younger sisters or female cousins could have been victims as well; I just wanted to be free.

The dreams of becoming a nurse and helping my family were far gone, and I was now just another girl from my community and a member of my family who would not amount to anything. I simply existed in the world that was created for me by my circumstances and had accepted my life as I saw it. I became more and more violent, and fights became more frequent, not just at school but in the streets as well. I became excellent at pretending while at home and was successful in living a double life. People in my immediate surroundings noticed the change from being a well-mannered child to an unruly teenager. It was a huge surprise to my teachers as well as myself when I obtained passes in seven ordinary-level subjects at the end of high school. The no-name God must have been on my side because the graduation ceremony had been canceled for that year due to a major brawl. I was not selected to participate in the ceremony anyway, but at least my parents would not know as it was canceled. Despite everything that was taking place in my life, for a moment a minute level of enthusiasm and expectancy was reignited when I realized I had seven subjects. For the first time in a long time, I thought about going to college and making something of my life. I reflected on my dream of becoming a nurse, making money, and taking care of my poor family. I remembered how I wanted to drive my own car, and in soberness of heart, I remembered the words spoken by my primary school teacher. However, this state of excitement was short-lived, as my father soon reminded me of the financial obligations of tertiary education and their inability to commit to helping me accomplish my dream on his measly salary. Disappointed and hurt yet another time in my life, I was forced to find work and fend for myself, and, again, the feeling of aloneness overwhelmed me. I became so angry inside with everyone around me that I felt as if I would have hurt someone. This was becoming too much for any one person to bear, and I felt I was always being robbed of an opportunity even though it may not have been intentional. As a result, I rebelled even more against my father, not understanding at the time that he was doing his best to make ends meet. How much more frustration, hurt, and setbacks could I take? When will I ever be given a chance to really live? Why does everything get taken away from me? Why does no one care? These are just a few of the questions I would ask, but an answer was never provided. By this time, my mother was no longer living in the one-bedroom board structure that constituted our family home, and, as usual, my father was only home on weekends, as he still had to maintain employment to provide for my three younger siblings, who I was now parenting. I found comfort in the party scene, and, as fate would have it, the struggles only multiplied when my father discovered I was pregnant at seventeen. In his disappointment and, to some extent, his lack of ability to provide for a fifth individual, I was asked to leave the house immediately, so I ended up on the streets with the daunting task of caring for myself and my unborn child. After several nights of having nowhere to sleep and my first real desire of desperately wanting to die but not having the guts to take my own life, I decided to move away to live with the father of my child. This was, by far, a bad decision, but being forced between a rock and a hard place, I had to make a choice, and I had to act fast. It was not as comfortable as I would have hoped to live in a residence with one room to spare for my brother-in-law and his family plus mine, but I had to make do with what I had, as it was much better than outside in the cold and I had no other option. My life became extremely difficult, especially since I couldn't find work at the time being in a strange environment, seventeen, and pregnant; I was solely dependent on the provisions of the baby's father. I took care of the house along with the other female who lived there, and I did my best to play my part. My life felt as if it was constantly heading on a downward spiral with every move I made. It was one poor decision after the next, and no matter how I tried to lift myself out of what seemed to be a witch's curse, I found myself right back where I started. After a while, I simply decided to accept what was handed to me and prepared myself for motherhood as best as I could.

Nine months went by quickly, it seemed, and my son was finally born in February of the following year. Though I had no idea what I would do from that point, I knew deep down that survival was crucial, as I now had someone else depending on me. I left the Victoria Jubilee Hospital several days after being treated for PIHTN (pregnancy induced hypertension) with a small person in my arms, not knowing what my next move was. As I traveled home alone with my new-born baby, I began to cry. I felt an overwhelming sense of being alone again and afraid. Everything began to flash across my mind like a large movie screen, and it only made me cry even more. I didn't care whether someone was looking; I just felt empty. The sun was scorching, and the pain I felt in my lower back and abdomen made the journey exhausting. I finally arrived home only to discover that the large wooden gate had been latched from the inside and the only way to get inside was to climb over. Not perturbed by this minor obstacle, I quickly executed my plan by placing the bag of clothing on the ground, making a cushion for the baby, and then placing the baby on the bag. I climbed over the gate, opened it from the inside, and finally, after a long wearisome day, made it to bed. I became a housewife and a mother in a very short time, and the only escape I had now was the substance that helped me to settle in my thoughts and gave me some semblance of focus. I couldn't party as much, as I didn't have anyone to watch the baby while I was out, so I settled for what I could whenever I got an opportunity. I was still breastfeeding but completely lacked knowledge of the consequences of drug and alcohol consumption on the infant. My selfish, rebellious, self-destructive ways propelled me into tattooing and body piercing, which became my diversion as well as my therapy.

About a year had passed since the birth of my son, and every day things became more strenuous psychologically, physically, and financially. I had no contact with my family except my father, whom I rarely ever spoke to. I didn't know where my mother was living at the time, the loneliness was becoming unbearable, and the drugs and alcohol were not enough to ease the pain anymore, as the more I used them, the more I craved. I thought of trying to get something more potent, but, of course, I hadn't yet identified a source. One day, while I was in the middle of doing my daily household chores, I received word that my mother had found a place to live, so I hurriedly made my way to visit her. I hadn't spoken to her in a while, and I was desperate to see a familiar face as well, no matter who it was. We were happy to see each other, and she was fascinated with the new addition to the family. We didn't talk much about our own lives and what was taking place, as that was always a very uncomfortable place. Instead, we talked about everything and everyone else. She mentioned old relatives who were sick and near death and the plans that were being made to distribute their belongings after they were gone. She also made small talk about what was taking place in her neighbourhood. Most of the time was spent fussing over the baby, but it was good to be in her presence for a while. I began to visit her more often at her new home. I'm not sure if I felt any better going back home, but after I returned, a relative of my son invited me to his church; I reluctantly agreed so he would stop asking, but, of course, I wasn't even sure how much I was interested in that. Eventually, I found that I actually liked it there, though I felt somewhat out of place. I had no clue if I would ever fit into this environment, as it felt foreign to what I had previously known as worship.

Despite this, I enjoyed the singing, and the preacher sounded as if he was making some sense, so every Sunday for about four months, I ensured I was in church. I would imagine myself singing on the choir in my beautiful maroon and gold robe, and I tried to make sense of the teachings about the God I never knew.

One day, the preacher asked the congregation if anyone wanted to give their lives to the Lord, not knowing exactly what that meant but thinking that it just may be better than anything else I had ever tried, I made my way to the front of the church, clutching my baby boy in my arms. The following night, I was baptized and instructed to run the race well. I could never run, as I never participated in any form of sporting activity at school, but I was okay with trying; after all, I didn't have anything to lose. This new routine was a good break for me. I couldn't quit the drugs and alcohol, but I found something I enjoyed and was motivated to one day wear the beautiful choir robe. It was not long before the pastor discovered I was involved in a common law relationship with the father of my child. He and the members of the church advised me that I could not get involved in the church activities, much to my dismay, as I was not married and was living a sinful life that was not pleasing to the Lord. This suddenly became a big problem, as I had nowhere else to go and I wanted to continue on my newfound path, but after sharing this with my consort, he decided we would get married. I asked my mother her opinion, and she encouraged me to get married even though I was only eighteen and had absolutely no clue what I was doing, so we did. We repeated vows we didn't understand; made promises we couldn't keep and created unrealistic expectations that we both could not live up to. I could now run the race, and, hopefully, I would win this one. As if my life did not have enough challenges, I learned that the only household income was lost. I laughed aloud with tears in my eyes, feeling that God did not play fair at all, that no matter what I did, I would always be on the losing end. I got upset at Him and decided that He wasn't any better than everyone else in my life, that I was chasing after something or someone I couldn't see that would only disappoint me, just like my family and everyone else did. I felt it was pointless to continue if this was how God was going to behave, so I stopped going to church and stopped praying. I sent a message asking my father if I could return home, as things were becoming extremely difficult and the family could not accommodate me for much longer without an income to assist with the expenses of the household. I had no idea how that would go and was in fact surprised when I heard that he agreed for me to return home. As a result, I wasted no time in packing the few items of clothing we had and left for the country with my family. Of course, I couldn't live in my dad's one-bedroom house, so I was assisted to build one beside his, and I settled with my family in a place I once knew as home. I soon landed a job as a counter clerk in a small hardware store and was able to feed my family, except this didn't sit well with my now unemployed husband, who eventually found other things and people to occupy his time. Not long after we moved back to the country, the fights began, and he would leave the house for days at a time, leaving me with no one to watch our son. The physical abuse was not affecting me as much as the psychological neglect and emotional deprivation. I was more than able to defend myself from the physical abuse, but every time I tried to maintain focus, the counterfeit blueprint of my life was presented before me, and it made me become more desperate to escape the pain inside.

The hate and anger I tried so hard to bury in my subconscious mind over the years began to resurface, and I was determined that no one would ever take advantage of me again. I became cold and callous, caring less and less about other people's feelings, feeling more and more hate toward everyone. I only saw the bad in people around me and told myself that even if the bad wasn't seen initially, it would surface eventually. I trusted no one. It didn't take long for things to escalate, and on the first anniversary of our wedding, we separated. I was tired of the cycle and needed to get out. When I arrived home from work later that evening, I felt a sense of relief, as I didn't have to face him anymore. I felt free. I propped myself down on the edge of the small double bed and smiled so hard my cheeks hurt. At nightfall, I lulled the baby to sleep and settled down for a peaceful night's rest.

Several weeks later, the street seemed awfully busy one particular evening; everyone was out of their houses waiting as if they had just received news that the rapture was coming. I didn't bother to stop to see what was taking place, as I felt it didn't concern me. As I continued along the roadway, I could hear the indistinct chatter in the background, and everyone seemed to stop talking and stare as I got closer to them. I felt they might have been discussing how I evicted my husband, as everything was community news for people who had nothing better to do, so I assumed that was the day's headline. I ignored the gathering, collected my son and went inside, where I would get settled in peace and quiet for the night. It all made sense now, or did it? I froze in the doorway in an awestruck moment as I stared in the big, empty space that was once my home, wondering where the few items of furniture and appliances had gone. Even the kitchen utensils were missing. That moment seemed like an hour as I stood there trying to piece the puzzle together, not realizing that my now ex-husband had returned to strip the house of everything I owned. I was so shocked that I could not find the will or common sense to shed a tear this time, as I was out of touch with reality for a brief period. I eventually pulled myself together as best as I could and sourced a piece of plywood and an old blanket that would become a makeshift bed for my son and myself for the next few weeks. That night, like many other nights I experienced as a child, sleep evaded me, and the thoughts competed for first place in my mind. The next morning, I asked my faithful neighbour to keep my son, and I went to work, well at least my body did. As I made my way to work, all I could think of was the scene I came home to the day before. I was still in disbelief and asked myself how any human being could be so evil. The questions continued to race through my mind like a flood as I tried to make it through my usual workday; I couldn't think straight. I was able to leave work a little earlier that day, so I went home. *Home,* I thought, as I slowly walked down the street trying to figure out what I would do next. It sure didn't feel like home right now, but I had to remain strong for my son. I did my usual picking up and pretended to be fine when I greeted the neighbour, went my way, and settled in our makeshift bed another night. *"I will recover from this,"* I told myself as I watched my little boy sleep soundly beside me. The next few days were the same, except I had come to terms with what had happened and began to plan my next move. I realized that my life obviously wasn't designed to be an easy one, but I was determined not to give up, if not for my own interest then for my son's well-being, so I continued as usual for the days to come.

They say lightning never strikes the same place twice, but they sure never said anything about hurricanes and tornadoes. Not only did I not have a bed to sleep on, but now I didn't have a roof over my head either or at least a part of it. Half of the roof was missing when I arrived home from work the next evening and, of course, this time the tears did not hesitate to make their way down my face, as I could not take the shame and hurt anymore. I cried helplessly as the pulsating beat of the hundreds of Congo drums in my head became louder and louder with every passing minute. I couldn't endure anymore. I had reached my breaking point now, and the piece of my sanity that was still intact was slowly being obliterated. I hadn't collected my son yet. For a short period of time, I forgot about him because I was lost in time and space, angry, desperate, and devastated. I had nowhere else to go; I really didn't know what to do this time. My neighbour, who was fully aware of what was happening all along, offered to keep my son for the night. I was ever so grateful, but since he was my only consolation, I politely rejected the offer and fetched him anyway. That night, I positioned the makeshift bed underneath the part of the roof that was still intact and cuddled my son until he fell asleep. As I sat beside my only reason to remain alive, I began to have flashbacks of the first moment tragedy struck in my life. I recounted every minute of every day and night since that summer when I was only eight years old. I remembered how my grandmother pretended to sleep beside me while life-stealing animals in the form of humans ripped my soul from within me. I remembered how my mother disregarded my account of what was happening when I finally had the guts at age fifteen to tell her about the nightmares. I remembered how my grandma accused me of lying and how one of my abusers inflicted several blows to my face while I slept after he was confronted by the mother of his child when word got out about his nasty secrets. I remembered how lonely my world was and how I tried to fill the empty spaces inside me by giving myself to the guys in my circle, drowning myself in alcohol and smoking my life away. I remembered how God never heard me—I remembered everything. I stared into the dark abyss with the tears streaming slowly down my face and my heart bleeding cold blood, made one last pull on the almost-finished cigarette, and leaned back against the wooden surface, finally nodding off to sleep before daybreak.

I was barely functioning at work by now due to the high degree of psychological stress I was undergoing and was soon asked to quit my job, which left me with absolutely no means to care for my child or myself. Where was God now? Night after night, we settled in our makeshift bed beneath the half side of the roof, and for the first time in a long time, I prayed. I prayed because I felt I had to remind God that I was still around just in case He got busy and forgot about me. I prayed because I had no money and could not continue to feed my child with unsweetened bush tea for breakfast, lunch, and dinner. I prayed because I didn't know what else to do and felt there was nothing more to lose at this point. I tried desperately to find work, but with no money to give to the neighbour to feed my son, it became increasingly difficult to leave him, as I was constantly concerned about the burden I was placing on this woman who was always willing to help, even though she didn't have much. On good days, I would braid someone's hair and earn enough money to buy dinner for a day or two, but obviously, this did not meet the needs of my small family. So, when I had the opportunity to work as a bartender, I gladly accepted it. It was not what I wanted but was far better than not having a job at all. At least I could put food on the table, or on the floor since I had no table. The difficulty of this was that I would be separated from my son, as I would now have to ask my mother to keep him since the hours would be inconvenient for my faithful neighbour.

CHAPTER 5

THE EFFECTS OF
CHILDHOOD SEXUAL ABUSE

Sexual abuse in a child can cause an immeasurable amount of overwhelming and intense feelings, resulting in harmful emotional and psychological effects on the victim. While everyone's experience and responses may be different, there are some responses that are believed to be quite common for all victims. Feelings of shame and guilt, as well as feelings of wanting to take one's own life, are only a few. I am no expert in the field nor have I undergone any formal study or research on the matter, but I can tell you from a place of personal experience that it is extremely difficult to even understand your own desires or to determine your own identity after abuse as a child, especially with no familial support. I know that childhood sexual abuse is no respecter of persons and can happen to anyone of any gender, from any social class or family background. I also know, based on literature I have examined, that people who are abused tend to engage in certain risky behaviors such as promiscuity and substance use/abuse. In my case, these were not done simply because I chose for them to happen, but to replace what I felt was stolen and fill the space that remained empty inside me, even years after my horrible experience.

IMMEDIATE EFFECTS

Guilt, shame, and self-hatred were some of the first emotions I identified with immediately after my experience.

Guilt

One of the most astounding effects I remember was the overwhelming sense of guilt I felt after the ordeal. As I entered my adult years and became more vocal about what happened, people said it was not my fault. Of course, they were right, but even though I knew this and usually shared it with other victims, I never applied it to myself. The abuse didn't make any sense to me as a child, as I was taught that adults were always right, and I must listen to them and obey them, so when these people violated my trust I could not make any sense of it. My sense of security and confidence in them was shattered because they were the ones who were supposed to keep me safe. So, to understand what happened, I figured I must have done something wrong. It was my fault, so I deserved whatever punishment was meted out to me because I assumed they were always right. As a child, I convinced myself that if I became invisible or was a *"good girl,"* it would not happen again. I believe this also intensified when my mother and grandmother eventually became aware but made no attempt to call it out for what it was. In addition to that, I didn't try to stop them, neither did I tell anyone about it for years; therefore, it was my fault that it continued. That was what I told myself for many years. I was afraid to resist or even tell my family about it in the initial phase, as I was warned not to. It took a long process of healing for me to realize that I was the victim and that I shouldn't be blamed for any of it, that it was their fault. It was very hard to feel completely free even after the actual abuse had stopped because this was something that walked around with me every day like my shadow. At the time, I was not aware of any resources, and, therefore, never had a support system. I felt isolated from family members and could only find strength in situations I could control. As a result, I became a bully and always fought my way out of situations, many times to my social detriment.

Shame

Many people may ask why I didn't come forward sooner, why wait until so many years later? Deep shame was one of the many reasons that kept me from coming forward. It was one of the most challenging things I have had to deal with, especially coming into my adult years, during my healing process and when I began contemplating a serious intimate relationship and marriage. I didn't want anyone to know about the abuse, especially the person I was going to marry. I was ashamed to let people know I had been contaminated, as that's how I felt. I learned a long, hard lesson that there was nothing I could ever have done to deserve the abuse and that there is always someone somewhere who is available to help me. However, at the time, I didn't feel comfortable talking to anyone about it and never even felt comfortable playing with the other kids. I felt dirty all the time and simply wanted to stay away from everyone. For several years during early adulthood, I continued to rationalize the feeling by tolerating poor treatment and even physical and verbal abuse from other men because the thought that I brought it onto myself or that I am not worthy to receive anything better was deeply embedded in me. I plunged myself sometimes unknowingly into situations that would lead to me getting hurt and became so comfortable in those unhealthy situations because I felt so unworthy, so much so that when someone genuinely tried to treat me right, it made me feel so uncomfortable. My dignity and innocence were stolen, my sense of pride was gone, and I felt that the abuse defined me as an individual, so I walked around all day thinking about it and feeling that it was the only thing that mattered in my life. What also added to the level of shame was when I eventually told members of my family, who at the time I didn't know was aware, and they refused to believe me, but instead made me out to be a liar and an evil person. I dug a dark hole for myself and made my residence there, afraid and ashamed to get out, no matter the cost.

Self-Hate

All I wanted to do was to die; my reason for living was completely reduced to me being a mere object of unhealthy pleasure for multiple deranged family members. Drunk or sober, rain or shine, every night they had access to me whether I liked it or not. Even though the actual abuse had ceased in my late teenage years, I still had to live with the feelings of depression and self-hate. Everything in my life, including my own children, became meaningless; the drugs and alcohol were no longer therapeutic, and suicide seemed to be the next best option on the table. The actual memories of the abuse were often buried way down in the subconscious, but the visible evidence was seen every day through my actions, which ranged from washing myself thoroughly and at length in the shower, giving myself to just about anyone who would accept me to satisfy an urge for instant pleasure, consuming bottles of alcohol, abuse of substance, and self-inflicting pain through the process of tattooing and piercings. It was very difficult, to say the least, to enjoy any form of intimacy as an adult. There was also an overwhelming sense of confusion about my own sexual identity, and I eventually blamed myself when my intimate encounters did not last beyond the moment, as I thought I must have had some type of negative aura that caused no one to want to stay around me for long. I thought any chance of a normal life was non-existent, and as I watched my life derail constantly, I became an expert in placing little or no value on myself. Powerless to bring any form of stability to my own life and those I had the responsibility to care for, my life moved from one crisis to the other in a never-ending cycle. I walked around every day bruised and broken, depressed and desperate to end my life. Counselors tried to diagnose me, but what I was experiencing could not be fixed by a series of therapeutic sessions or even medication. The constant process of rolling back the curtains of memories in those counseling sessions only intensified the will to die. After two suicide attempts, I was determined that the third one wouldn't fail. It's hard when someone feels alone in the world and that no one cares, and, at times, there may be persons who are genuinely looking out for them and willing to make all types of sacrifices but being blinded by the mask of depression makes it almost impossible to discern. I came to know and accept later in life that Jesus had never left me or forsaken me, but at the time I felt like nobody's child.

LONG-TERM EFFECTS

Promiscuity

I was making good money at my job in the bar, and I was enjoying the lifestyle, no commitments; I was simply having a good time, and it felt liberating. Or so I thought. At that time, I felt I should try everything at least once. I was totally oblivious to the fact that that job actually set the stage for a whole different turn of events that would eventually cause me to go farther on a downward slope with the devil by my side, so I blindly accepted it as a blessing. I was doing well, and sales were pretty good; furthermore, I soon began to entertain the male patrons with small talk, which would sometimes lead to a large tip, a trip on the dance floor, and often even their homes. I never saw the dangers crouching at my doorstep, but saw it as an easy, enjoyable way to make money. Marijuana and alcohol once again became paramount to maintain a certain high to perform my job well, and in no time, those male patrons became not just customers but targets and goals for my financial and personal gratification. I had absolutely no intention of developing or maintaining a lasting, stable relationship, as I was afraid of the requirements of committing emotionally. I decided I just wanted to focus on getting myself back on my feet and securing some type of stability for my child. I soon lost count of my sexual partners. I felt I had to always find someone new. The thing about this job was that I went in with a perfect plan. I needed to get in, make my money, and get out. I had every intention of finding another job as a clerk and taking my son back to live with me, but it didn't happen that way. I was pretending to have the time of my life, looking for new ways and people to make me happy, but I was killing myself slowly inside.

He was just another who caught my eye. I watched him as he laughed and engaged in light conversation with his guests at the party and thought to myself that this would be a good conquest for the evening. Growing weary of deliberating much longer, I summoned my friend and asked him to tell my new target to meet me a short distance away from the crowd. It didn't take long before he got to the designated location, and after a quick introduction and a few formalities, I began my mission, which was accomplished before the end of the evening. This was the case with many others before him; therefore, I didn't give a second thought about whether I would see him again, as I had already received all that I wanted. It was a great evening, and I would simply go back to my regular routine tomorrow. I told myself I was never ashamed of what I was doing, neither did I pay attention to what people would say about me. By the time I was in my mid-twenties, I imagine I may have slept with over thirty men. Truthfully, most of those encounters were filled with disappointment; maybe a few were pleasurable occasions. I didn't initially intend to sleep with so many. I just always felt empty, and after the encounters, I would end up feeling worse than before. It was like an addiction, a disease that had no cure. I knew I needed to get out, but I did not have the will or the courage to do so. Some days all of this would be fun and exhilarating and affirming, yet other days it was mostly terrifying. When the lights were off, my clothes in a pile on the floor, and I was supposed to be the most intimate with someone, the feelings that rushed in left me feeling worthless and paralyzed. But still, I pressed repeat and did it all over again, slowly killing the remainder of my soul.

Lesbianism

We began to spend a lot of time together and would even babysit each other's children. She was now married to the father of her last child, but her husband was always away working out of town, leaving her with a little too much time on her hands. Deep down, she knew he had another life outside the home, and while she never expressed that she was bothered about it, she never seemed too happy either. Maybe she found comfort in having the freedom to party as she liked and not have the real demands of marriage or maybe she didn't want anyone to know how badly she was hurting. Whatever it was, she did a great job of maintaining her sanity and portraying that upbeat, happy personality that everyone knew her for. She was great at being who she was, and I always wondered how she could maintain such a positive attitude, knowing that her life was breaking apart. I, on the other hand, was always vocal about my feelings and never hesitated to express them to my new friend.

My new live-in boyfriend and supplier of narcotics and alcohol searched for ways to hustle; his ultimate goal was to eventually join his daughter's mom in England while mine was to survive by any means necessary, including having him around for as long as was required. My female friend wasn't very fond of him, as she believed he was an opportunist, but I was not perturbed, as there was no commitment, no love, just an understanding for a temporary period. I never realized that the reason she hated him so much was not necessarily because he was a crook and a womanizer but because she, too, was attracted to me. And all the while I was pouring out my heart in grief, she was secretly anticipating the perfect opportunity to lure me into her love nest.

Most days, we sat at the back of the yard on the stairway, as the trees provided a nice canopy of shade for us to relax and talk. This day was no different, except that it was a very overwhelming one for me, as was the norm from time to time. While I was trying to negotiate my next move, she had already decided on hers. She slipped her arm up toward my upper back and gently pulled my head toward her so that it rested on her shoulder. There was absolutely nothing weird about this, as she was just being a friend, but when I attempted to complete my next sentence, I was prevented from getting the last few words out as I felt her pressing her lips against mine. I sat there with the tears still streaming down my cheeks, eyes wide open in complete astonishment, uncertain about whether I should bitch slap her or kiss her back. I was never exposed to this kind of compassion, but also knew this was the only person I had in my corner. As a million thoughts raced through my mind and I began to feel something moving in my stomach, I closed my eyes and got lost in the moment. We never spoke about what happened that day, but there was a nonverbal line of communication open between us that suggested it was okay, so we began spending more and more time together not just as friends anymore but as lovers. Since no one in the neighbourhood knew about us, we ensured that it remained a secret. This lasted for quite some time and somehow, subconsciously, inspired the unnatural desire for more women. I began to see girls and women in a different light. Since I have always been on the more aggressive side in my sexual conquests, I went in search of new companions. I soon forgot about my most recent heterosexual relationship and in no time completely lost my appetite for the opposite sex; becoming the exact thing I hated. I got involved with multiple female partners with no concern for their feelings. I was on a selfish pursuit to happiness, or at least my interpretation of it. I did not know I was simply opening the door to more hurt and hate, as I was lost in a desire that was filling my flesh but destroying my soul. My old friend became very jealous after a while, as she saw the new "friends" coming by my house, so she came by less and less. I was free to live my life, and I did just that; partying, smoking, drinking, and sleeping with a different girl almost every night. My dad despised my behaviour, but I didn't care about what he thought. The people in the community began to talk about me, but because that was the custom where I was from, my focus was on having fun at any cost. I soon became isolated from my family. I was heading toward a deadly path, a downward spiral to hell, but I was so blind by hurt and a selfish desire to gratify the emptiness inside that I couldn't see it.

CHAPTER 6

MY JOURNEY TO HEALING

It is ironic how the place of pain can be the very place used by God to bring healing. I was having the time of my life when I heard that my estranged grandmother was sick and in the hospital. Since I wasn't working, I went to visit her and help her around the house for a few days. I gave a lot of consideration to how I would feel going back to my grandmother's house, but I knew I wasn't afraid of my abusive family members anymore. I was more focused on going, as I heard she was seriously ill. I didn't intend to stay more than a week anyway. As a result, I did not pack more than enough clothing to last that long. I left for town to visit my grandmother for the first time in about ten years. When I arrived, I noticed that the yard looked the same as it did ten years ago, except there were no happy children, no new relatives, and no one waiting for the evening meal. The fruit trees were scanty, with little or no blossoms, and the shop shelves were empty. Warrior Princess was lying in the same bed, very weak and with very little ability to speak. No other relative was in sight, not that I wanted to see them anyway. I got settled and immediately began to tidy the house, as it was unkempt, and people were coming to visit. I swept the yard, made some soup for her, and finally settled down for the evening on the veranda. Early the next morning, I got up and cleaned the shop, and then I went shopping for items to sell, as my grandmother was too weak and the stock for her shop was depleted. About day four, she began to move around in the yard a little, but she still couldn't manage her everyday tasks, so I operated the shop and did the household chores for her. I saw a few of my old friends and acquaintances, and even though they seemed to have fond memories of me, things were not the same from my perspective; I was cold and unfriendly toward them. I contacted a cousin I was close to who became my party partner. I really didn't miss being at home, and my abusive family members still stared at me, but they made no attempt to even speak to me this time. Being here brought back a lot of sad memories, but I had become so hardened with hate by now that it didn't matter. I would quickly dismiss the thoughts and pretend as if they never existed; well, in my mind, they really didn't.

I was going about my regular routine one afternoon when a middle-aged woman came to the shop to make a purchase. I had never seen her before and really wasn't in the mood for light conversation, but the woman persisted in asking me questions as if she was trying to get to know me. I was skimpily attired as usual, and the expression on the woman's face suggested she didn't approve of my style of dress. I thought that was good and might cause her to leave the shop quickly, but it didn't. She said she never realized that my grandmother had such big grandchildren and asked how she has never seen me for the greater part of nine years since she lived next door. She was quickly sacked with blunt responses, but she either did not get the message that I wasn't interested, or she was determined to get the information she wanted. The conversation lasted longer than was welcomed, and at the end, the woman asked what I was doing with myself, referring to my career choice. I told her nothing at the moment, thinking that would be her last question, but the woman insisted on asking how many subjects I had and what I aspired to become in life. I was beginning to get annoyed with all those questions from a total stranger, but because she was a mature lady who could have been my mother, I extended common courtesy and obliged her by answering. The woman finally purchased her goods and left the shop, much to my relief.

The next day, I was sitting in the shop when suddenly the woman appeared and stood at the counter. I murmured under my breath and wondered what she wanted this time. The woman simply presented me with a legal-size paper and left. On closer examination, I recognized that she had listed several schools of nursing in and around town with the requirements for admission and contact information. I stood in amazement as I asked myself why on God's earth this woman seemed to have such a vested interest in me, a total stranger. We were not related and never even knew each other before the first time she came into the shop. I blindly found my seat, but with my jaws still falling to the floor, I went through the paper in detail, wondering to myself if it was even still possible to pursue a career in nursing at the age of twenty-six after all that had transpired. I barely even remembered having that dream to become a nurse, and I didn't feel I could live up to the standards of a respectable professional. I didn't feel I had what it took to go back to school and do well. I felt I had lost all hope of making something of myself, and in that moment, I decided it would be a waste of my time.

I placed the paper in an old hardcover book that seemed to have existed before Jesus' birth and conditioned my mind that this was the life for me. This was where the buck stopped. I spent two more days filling in for my grandmother, and I never saw the woman again. As my grandma regained her strength and could now resume her role as shopkeeper, I packed my bag, intending to catch the first bus out to the country the next morning.

Later that night, my grandma reached for an old hardcover book as a half-drunken man came to ascertain his outstanding bill, and I immediately remembered that I was presented with a thought-provoking, possibly life-changing opportunity. I took out the paper and perused it again as if seeing it for the first time. I didn't tell my grandmother what had happened but decided I would at least call a few of the numbers and see what it would lead to. I got the information and was told to drop off an application by a certain deadline to start school the following September.

I did as was instructed and went by the school, and as the months slowly dragged by, I waited for the call. About 2:30 that afternoon, the phone rang, and a female voice asked for me by name. The lady identified herself and said she was calling from the University of the West Indies and that I should come to write an English exam that was compulsory for admission. This was surreal; I hung up the phone and laughed. I had no money to travel back and forth and couldn't deprive my poor grandmother of the little she had. That same evening, as sure as the night sky, the middle-aged neighbour came to the shop again. I thought to myself for the first time that maybe God had been sending her. The woman asked me how things were going with the application and whether I had heard anything yet. I told her I received a call and that I had an exam to write the following day. I didn't mention that I had no money, as I didn't want her to feel sorry for me. After a much lighter conversation than the last one, the woman handed me an envelope, wished me good luck on my exam, and left. As she left, I opened the envelope to find I had enough money to travel to and from school and purchase refreshments on the way. I didn't cry this time, but I became even more confused about why this woman was being so helpful. I wondered how she knew I would need the money, as I didn't speak to anyone about it. The thought of God providing a way out for me came to mind, but I chuckled deep in my throat and thought I must be crazy to think God would waste His time on me. I made my way to the school that morning and did my best on the exam; curious about what would transpire. I stayed in town for a little while longer.

It was now August and more than two months since I left home for a trip that was intended to last only a few days. I still had not received a call back from the school, and several thoughts began to rush through my mind. I began to tell myself that I knew this was going to happen and blamed myself for trying. *Why did I think I would pass it anyway?* I thought, as that familiar feeling of disappointment crept in.

I didn't care about staying in town, but I didn't care about going back home anymore either.

About a week later, the woman next door returned to ask me for an update on the process. I wasn't too happy to see her, as she was the one who set me up for disappointment. I wondered why this woman didn't just leave me alone, but I knew she wouldn't. I explained that I took the exam but failed it since I had not received a follow-up call. The woman encouraged me to remain hopeful, as I still had time. About the first week in September, as I was preparing to go home, the woman called to tell me she had called the school and she was informed that a package was there waiting to be collected for the past two weeks. I was beside myself with excitement beyond my ability to express; I was good enough after all. I smiled at myself, and a glimmer of hope came over me instantaneously. I had no clue how I would make it through three years of study with no job and no savings. I didn't receive any word from the student's loan bureau and even securing guarantors was a task, but I did not focus on that, I was invincible; I was going to university, and that's all that mattered.

I started school with the help of the woman next door one week late, as I didn't receive my package on time, but the registration process was still in progress. I got busy and filled out the necessary paperwork, selected my courses, and officially became a university student with absolutely no fees. It was a great challenge to travel every day, especially with no means of income except what I got from the next-door neighbour. I soon remembered I had a relative living closer to school, so I told my mother to ask if I could stay at the relative's house, as it would be cheaper to travel to and from. She agreed, and so I moved from my grandmother's place to her home. I was never made aware of the living arrangements until after the move. I was informed that I would share a bed with my younger cousin and be required to contribute several thousand dollars per month to assist with the bills. I had no idea how this would be possible, as I was still trying to determine how my tuition was going to be paid.

By the second semester, I was contacted by the loan bureau but was told I needed more guarantors to secure the funds for school. I had no idea who this would be, so I called on everyone I knew. Two relatives stepped in and offered to help, and I was introduced to a man by my youngest sister, a close friend who was willing to sign on the loan as long as I would meet with him. After a quick introduction and a short semi-formal interview, he signed for the first two years. Things were definitely looking positive now, and I was determined to make it work. I was encouraged by the words of the Prophet:

> *Isaiah 49:15-16: "Can a woman forget her nursing child, and not have compassion on the son of her womb? Surely they may forget, yet I will not forget you. See, I have inscribed you on the palms of My hands; Your walls are continually before Me."*

I ensured I committed myself to study at length every day, as I was in no position to pay for a re-sit, if I failed a course. Of course, I couldn't purchase books and had to depend on different sources to gather information for research and other assignments. As such, I would spend hours at a time in the school's library searching the internet for journals and other materials. At times, I grew very tired and would often fall asleep at the computer desk until one of the attendants awakened me and encouraged me to go to my room. I was living on campus by this time, as I never thought it made sense to be paying for a couch to sleep on when I could have a room for myself. My cousin needed her room, and the only option I had was to sleep on the couch or move out. The money I was contributing to the household could have paid for a small room on campus, and that made it easier for me to get to study meetings and classes since I would save on transportation cost, so I made the best decision and moved out. My children would hardly see me now, as I couldn't afford to travel back and forth while in school, and this made me sad at times. I found assurance in the fact that I would be able to finish school soon and secure profitable employment, so I could have them with me, and I looked forward to it.

I still maintained my salesperson reputation from high school, except this time I was not selling drugs but food items and anything else I could get my hands on to help with my daily expenses. I also received assistance from the woman who helped me to get into school and ensured I kept her up to date with my progress, as she often reminded me that that was the only thanks she desired. With the help of God, I maintained an excellent average on my transcript despite all the challenges, even though I gave no credit to Him. I found it very difficult to stop partying, smoking, and using alcohol, as it had now become a habit I was having great difficulty breaking, even though I wanted to change that. I knew it was harmful to my health and felt awful after I would hide from my college mates to get high. I was also involved in a long-term relationship with a female colleague, a relationship I planned to maintain after graduation, though everything inside me kept telling me it was wrong. Like the unnamed woman at the well, I needed my spiritual thirst to be quenched; I needed to receive something that would satisfy me once and for all, something that would erase the guilt associated with the mistakes I have made and help me focus on the future ahead of me. I needed the water that was living, the change that would not only impact me but those I would eventually tell about this Man. Like the woman at the well, I needed to be transformed eternally by the power of Christ. I needed to be saved.

A drastic turn of events took place one night as I was on my way to a party with my cousin. I passed a large tent crusade in the square. It was early, and I had to wait for my other friend who was running late, so I stood outside listening to the singing and watching the people dance in the Holy Ghost. Despite having some experience with the church, though very short lived, I didn't want to go in, as I was more focused on going about my business, plus I was not appropriately attired for a church setting. I simply saw it as buying time and never assumed it was my appointment with the Lord. I stood there for a while, and as the memory of when I used to attend church several years before flashed across my mind, I hurriedly made my way to the outside corner, which led to the exit of the property, as I refused to come face to face with my conscience. As I was about to leave, the preacher beckoned me to come under the tent. I pretended I didn't know he was referring to me and turned to walk away. He called out to me again by describing the color of my outfit. I still insisted on not going, but he was persistent and said God had given him a message for me. I shook my head and attempted to exit from the side but found it extremely difficult to leave. Something was happening that I was unwilling to embrace, and I was very upset with myself for feeling so vulnerable. I did not like the feeling of being stripped of myself at all, and as the preacher gave me the *"message"* I felt I was being totally exposed. The next thing I knew, I was at the front of the church, weak and helpless, crying to God and asking Him to save me from myself. That night I understood what it meant to give my life to the Lord for the first time, and I was ready to do so. I came to terms with what was in front of me, with the lies I was telling myself and those the enemy had told me, and I surrendered my life to Jesus once and for all.

I had no idea what time my friend arrived, as I left the meeting after my encounter and went back to my room. I made up in my mind that I was going to serve the Lord, and over the course of several months, He revealed how He had been providing for me, how He had been there all the while when I felt he wasn't. Somehow, I knew in my heart that it was true, and I felt a deep sense of gratitude. I soon found a church to attend and became a part of a family I never had. The journey was still difficult at times because I still struggled with drugs and alcohol use, the hate I had for the male species, as well as my feelings for females. I sometimes asked God how He allowed all the bad things to happen to me and why He never protected me from it, but I wasn't sure He would answer or maybe I wasn't listening. I had some good and bad days, but I was hopeful that my life had taken a turn for the better. I began attending counseling sessions that were set up for me by the church, but I didn't see how it was helping me to get over the issues. I found that I got angrier and upset during and after these sessions than I would normally be otherwise. I felt I was wasting my time as well as that of the facilitator, as I couldn't understand how a man who has never experienced what I had could tell me how to fix it with methods I couldn't identify with. I felt it was superficial and a poor attempt to help me, so after a while, I stopped showing up for these meetings.

About two years had passed, and I was still active in church, but there were some things that still hadn't changed. I wasn't using drugs anymore, but I still consumed alcohol occasionally, and I still had a desire to be with a woman, although I wasn't acting on it. I became frustrated with myself and how hard it was to get past all that was staring me in the face. I didn't understand how to deal with all the feelings I was having; the feelings of unforgiveness, resentment, anger, and hate. The relationship with my dad was the only one that improved while I was studying, as he often called to check on me and encourage me during my studies, something that never happened in all the years I knew him. Apart from my somewhat unstable relationship with God, things were looking and feeling better.

CHAPTER 7

WHERE AM I NOW?

Soaking in every word from the guest speaker and being swollen with pride to see my family, including my father, sitting in the audience, I stood there with a broad smile on my face thanking God for how He had brought me to this point. I still had a long way to go, but I was grateful for the dramatic change that was made in my life and the compelling assurance that He was with me. I thought about the young girl I used to be and how I tried to determine my own future by blindly accepting what people said and what I thought about myself. I thought of how many times I gave up on my dream and accepted the lies the enemy told me. My grandmother's next-door neighbour and new boyfriend, who were also present, expressed how proud they were of me as well. The neighbour expressed that her mission was now finally accomplished as she saw me standing in my graduation gown receiving my degree, for which I was awarded high honors. I was proud of myself for being able to be an example to my two children and grateful to God for making something out of nothing. As I sat there, my focus shifted and was no longer on how God kept silent when I needed Him but instead on how He allowed me to have those experiences, so I could see His hand in my life bringing me out. I immediately thanked Him for not giving up on me all those years. It is never easy when we are in the situation to see the positive, as the situation causes a lot of hurt and pain, but I learned through the years that God never waste a test; He never allows us to experience anything nor take us anywhere that He cannot use to bring glory to His name. All the trials I had experienced as a child, a teenager, and a young adult were always part of His wonderful plan to fashion my life into a great example for other girls and women who were not yet at the place where I was.

Having been given the opportunity to look back over my own life, I can thank God that He kept me through it all; I can truly say He has never left me, even though many times during and even after those years of terror I questioned His presence and became angry at Him for His inactivity. I remember when Jesus was asked in the book of John why this man was born blind; they questioned whether it was something he did or maybe something his parents did that resulted in this deficiency, but Jesus' response made something clear that I can now relate to my own circumstances. He explained that neither the man nor his parents did anything wrong, but that the man was born blind, so the glory of God could be demonstrated in his life. Similarly, there are times when you may face trying circumstances in your life and have no control over the outcome. You may find yourself asking *Why me Lord* or *Why would God allow this to happen to me?* It is not because He doesn't love you. In fact, He loves you so much and has such great confidence in you that He chose you to carry such a burden. Jesus was God's only son whom He loved so much, yet He sent Him to earth to die for you and me, even though He knew no sin. When Jesus was in the Garden praying, He expressed His desire to not have to endure the cross, having foreknowledge of exactly what He would face. He asked the Father to let the cup pass from

Him, but then he said, *"Not My will Father but Your own."* He knew that although it would have been so painful, despite the humiliation and the hurt, the torture and the horror of a long slow death, it was God's will and for God's glory. Therefore, He willingly endured His cross.

James wrote to encourage us to count it all joy when we face different situations in life that cause us pain. It's not because we are so foolish or lack emotion or that we are expected to be robotic and not feel sad or discouraged when we face these issues, but because he wants us to recognize that our trials are never about us but for those we will encounter in the future. They are to strengthen us and make us wiser, so we may be able to strengthen others and help them navigate their way to their positions of victory. This has now become a powerful source of comfort and assurance for me as I embrace my own story and gladly share it with others to encourage them about dealing with their struggles. I have found the strength to move beyond the shame, the guilt, and the self-hate and come to a place of understanding and acceptance that I was chosen to endure this hardship, so God could use my life's journey to bring others to a place of healing and hope and bring glory to His name.

I was later introduced to a powerful man of God who prayed with me for hours and coached me through the process of receiving complete spiritual deliverance from the things that had me bound. I forgave my mother, grandmother, and my abusers for everything they did and did not do. I was able to truly speak positively in their lives and mean it, and for the first time in many years, I was able to sincerely tell my mother those three dreaded words I held back for so long—*I love you.*

This man of God invited me to minister with him and a group of believers on the mission field. This was completely new to me, but it soon became my passion, and I used it as a platform to share my life with others as I watched God truly turn my life around. Though I still had some inhibitions in sharing some details of my life story with others, I was happy to tell the world how He had changed me. I ministered in churches every chance I got, as I was now at the place of victory, believing I was special to God and that all that He had allowed to happen was for the divine purpose He wanted to bring out in my life. I was grateful to God for where He had brought me from and all the things He had taken me through. I was thankful that He kept His promise to never leave me nor forsake me. I was grateful that I found Him. Had I not allowed God to heal me, I would not have been able to minister to so many young women whom I have seen grow in their own personal walk with the Lord. I was so angry at God and everyone else at one point that I couldn't see this. I was so consumed with my own feelings that I failed to realize that others around me may have been having similar experiences. I was so blinded by unforgiveness and filled with hate and a selfish desire for revenge that I couldn't understand the purpose God was birthing in me.

Many times, we lose sight of, or don't even know the ultimate reason we were born. It is, however, God's desire that every one of us identify and walk according to the plan He has set out for us, but we will never come to the awareness of this unless we are walking in a meaningful relationship with Him. For this reason, the enemy of our souls takes every opportunity to distract, discourage, and deter us from this path so we may never fulfill our God-given potential. The longer we hold on to pain and hurt from the past, the longer we will inflict emotional and even physical damage onto ourselves, and I recommend that you make every effort to find that place in God where He freely gives us the grace to forgive. Believe me, that was not at all easy, and traditional counselling could not help me to accomplish that based on where I was. I'm not suggesting that professional counseling is not effective, as it has been proven without question to be a very effective way to deal with the effects of abuse and to overcome the challenges presented as a result. However, my road to recovery took a different direction, and that is what I can speak about. I developed a meaningful relationship with Jesus Christ and began to study the Word of God daily. I was taught through the Word about my identity as a child of God and the authority that had been given to me by Jesus to overcome anything at all that came to destroy me. Over time, I fully embraced this knowledge and am now able to walk with my head held high, knowing who I am and to Whom I belong and having the ability to defy the odds from a God-motivated standpoint.

As a believer in Christ, I have seen a major growth in my personal walk with Him. I have been able to literally feel relieved from the self-blame that I inflicted because of the abuse. I realized after many years of suffering and being overcome with hate and anger toward my family that it was, in fact, destroying me in every way, to the point where I attempted suicide three times. Before this, I could never speak to my mother without thinking how much I hated her. On one occasion, I was told how much I resembled her, and all I could do was cry uncontrollably. Through the grace of God and what he had implanted in me through His Word as well as help from other strong believers in Christ who prayed me through my deliverance, I was able to rise above all the negative, emotional bondage and release my family and myself from the prison of unforgiveness. I can speak to all of them, holding no grudges, and will now willingly assist in any way I can to make their lives better, as I believe they are the ones who truly need healing and an encounter with Jesus.

I have also been able to develop and maintain a healthy intimate relationship and a stable marriage and can now focus my efforts on strengthening my family. My children have been made aware of my struggles and are enlightened about the reality of the issue and how to help prevent this occurrence in their own lives as well as to identify signs in those close to them. I have also been empowered to channel my energy into positive things like working in ministry and furthering my education and fulfilling my childhood dream of becoming a registered nurse. This was, by far, one of the most physically challenging goals to meet, as I was unemployed with no financial assistance and two children. I was mostly dependent on the kindness of one woman, whom I believe God sent directly in my life to help me along the way. I now understand that it is never God's intention to hurt us, as His Word says, He desires that we prosper as our soul prospers. In fact, He only allows us to experience the things He knows will produce resilience and strength in us, things that will make us out to be a fighter and to build courage, teach us wisdom and patience, and, most importantly, glorify Him as we see His mighty hand working out these various situations in our lives. One of the greatest accomplishments in my life, apart from coming to know the Lord, was to graduate from university, as many people, including myself, believed it was not possible. I am now liberated to live and to speak.

It took me about three months after graduation, much less than average, to get my first job as a nurse, fulfilling the dream I had from primary school. My children and I are now under the same roof, and I am married to a phenomenal man of God. I learned that what the enemy intends to use to harm us is the same thing God uses to bring out the best in us, and so I am eternally grateful that He chose me to endure all the things I had. I have since spent many years before the Lord growing in His grace and maturing in the call on my life and soon found that He was calling me into women's ministry. Everywhere I went, I would encounter women and girls who have had the same or similar experience I had. I could share with them how God had brought me out by His mighty hand

and how my life was now all I had imagined it to be and more. I found joy in sharing with others the things that once made me ashamed and guilty or caused me pain. I am happy to tell someone that He can do it for them because He did it for me.

My husband and I decided to dedicate our whole lives to doing God's work and enhancing His kingdom, and it is all because of where God had taken us from. The blueprint of my life was now rewritten, and as my action steps are implemented each day, I see life-changing decisions being made by those I have the honour of ministering to. Today, I can truly say God is a shelter in a stormy night and a strong tower in which I can hide. If you are or have been in situations such as myself, it is not too late for you to be completely healed and set free by the blood of Jesus. There are many stories in the Scripture where we see Jesus restoring and using people who were once considered unusable. That is the reason Jesus came to earth and died so that people like you and I, who were once outcasts in the eyes of our society, can be completely transformed and become a dangerous weapon for Him. It is not too late for you to open up your heart and allow Him to come in and change you from the inside. There is no terror or anxiety that God doesn't comprehend. He sees the wars that rage within us and has an incessant provision of strength for those who submit to His authority. Through His Word, we can learn how to face those things that oppose us without fear, rising above anything or anyone we are threatened by.

If you are a born-again believer, ask the Lord to empower you with His Holy Spirit as you transition from a place of hurt and pain to a place of victory. If you are not yet saved, and you would like to experience the transforming power of Jesus Christ, I invite you to take a few moments to surrender your life to Jesus, so He can heal you; mind, body, and soul. Romans 10:9-10 says, *"That if you confess with your mouth the Lord Jesus and believe in your heart that God has raised Him from the dead, you will be saved. For with the heart one believes unto righteousness, and with the mouth confession is made unto salvation."* Salvation is made available only through the blood of Jesus Christ to all those who will accept it simply by sincerely making this declaration:

Father in heaven, I believe in my heart that Jesus Christ is Lord.

I believe that He died for my sins and rose again and is alive today.

Lord Jesus, I ask You to come into my life and change me into a new person.

I give You my life in return for what You have done on the cross.

Be my Lord and my Saviour, I pray, in Jesus' name.

Thank you for saving me.

If you said this prayer and meant it, then you are now a child of God. The Bible says if any man be in Christ, he is a new creature; old things are passed away and behold all things are become new (2 Corinthians 5:17).

Congratulations!

The process of healing has begun, and your life is about to change for good as you walk in complete obedience to the Word of God.

CHAPTER 8

WHAT ABOUT YOU?

I may not know you personally, but on some level, we both know shame, guilt, pain, and struggle, and we both have come to a time in our lives when we feel like we should throw in the towel. I want to tell you today that you are not alone. Even when you feel no one understands how you feel, what you have gone through, or what you are going through, someone out there somewhere is fighting this very same battle. I know your experience may be different from mine, but the hurt is the same, and the ability to heal resides in the same powerful, loving God. He created you fearfully and wonderfully in His image and His own likeness, and He wants to heal you; body, mind, and soul, if you let Him. For God to do this, He will need to access those parts of you through submission, even when you feel disappointed and discouraged. As you take this journey with me, here are a few things I want to bring to your attention. There are several principles in Scripture that we can apply to help us have the assurance that harmful situations are not necessarily the end of our fate. One of my favorites is Isaiah 54:17:

> *No weapon formed against you shall prosper, and every tongue which rises against you in judgment You shall condemn. This is the heritage of the servants of the LORD, and their righteousness IS from Me, Says the LORD.*

If we recognize that these are simply weapons of Satan, then we will be better equipped to nullify his efforts and triumph over him. I remember when I was first made aware of the fact that to come alive again, I must do this. I remember how difficult it was for me to accept that I must forgive my family, especially my mother, since she was the one with the greater responsibility to protect me from harm. It felt like an impossible task considering I was barely able to remain in the same room with her for more than 24 hours. I couldn't have a civil conversation with her; I wasn't able to tell her I loved her. I hated her so much that when someone told me I resembled her, I became so angry and wanted to distance myself from them. The effects were real, and they were affecting every area of my life, including my sanity.

I soon realized I couldn't do it alone and was very much dependent on people who God had placed in my life to help me transition to the next level in Him. Below, I will outline the steps I used over time to move from a place of hate and pain to a place of passion and purpose.

1. **Acknowledge the fact** – I had to accept that the situation had already taken place and that I probably could not have prevented it. There is absolutely no way I could go back in the past to change anything, and even if I could, I would not have learned the valuable lessons I did. Every experience, both positive and negative, every struggle and circumstance is for a purpose and has a lesson to be learned. It may not seem that way initially and may seem overwhelming, especially when there is no support from family and friends, but if you *stay focused, you will see that there was an intended purpose for the pain you were chosen to endure.* As the old adage goes,

"There's no point crying over spilled milk." I understood that remaining at a place of hurt and defeat would only cause more harm than good for me and those around me and would definitely interfere with my ability to reach my intended destination.

2. **Seek God** – I had to spend endless nights in prayer to find out God's plan and the direction He was leading me into. I had to ask Him about the why, where, when, and the how of my story. There is no point in going if God has not sent you with a message, so it is imperative to know the move of God and the season of your life at any given point. It's not just about sharing, but there are several times when I had to literally seek God to find out which area of my life to share based on the people He sent me to, as not every part would have been relevant to every single individual. Knowing the voice of God and being sensitive to the move of the Spirit is paramount in reaching people at the core and being able to truly minister to them according to the need. So, begin seeking God now, for He will never fail you. Even when all you and others seem to see is failure, you will always have a secure and solid place on which to stand.

3. **Allow yourself to hear** – God spoke to Elijah on top of the mountain in a still, small voice. That voice is always speaking to us every moment of every day; sometimes we fail to listen and other times we fail to

hear. It is unfortunate that many of us, like me, were not raised with this truth. God's vested interest in us as unique individuals is what makes us special, and no matter what we may discover or are made to believe about ourselves, His word that was spoken about us before this world was formed is what stands. Maybe we are afraid because others told us we weren't good enough and that we will not amount to anything, but everything inside of you is good and perfectly designed for God's glory, and only you can accomplish what He has ordained for you. So, listen attentively to that still small voice so He can lead you onto the path of hope and complete healing.

4. **Seek help** – I am fully aware that I am not the only one who has ever gone through hurtful situations; there are others with an enormous amount of experience of how God can use an individual who has been at their worst. It is with this knowledge that I sought mature believers to strengthen me through prayer and encouragement in my walk with the Lord and in identifying my purpose and fulfilling it. My husband also played a major role in this season, as he always prayed for me and encouraged me as I found myself in God. Having this type of support system makes it easier, as I had the assurance that I was not alone, and it gave me courage in the difficult times.

5. **Know your worth** – You are the apple of God's eye and you are very important to Him, unique and gifted in every way, even though at times you may feel alone and isolated and often feel you're not good enough. With all of this going on in your mind, take time for self-reflection through God's eyes by reading His Word and learning what He has to say about you. Listen to His voice and comfort yourself through the sadness and celebrate and embrace the positive moments you have. If you have not already started this habit, I encourage you to get a journal and write about everything you experience on a day-to-day basis. As you write, God will use the opportunity to speak softly into your spirit those words of love, assurance, and healing.

6. **Own it** – Though your circumstance is not necessarily unique to you, it is your story, your process that you have been through, and no one can discredit that. Everyone's destination with God is the same, but everyone's journey is different. So, I had to learn to embrace the things He used to refine me. *What makes you who you are? What makes you happy? What is your drive and motivation? What are you good at? What are your interests? What do others admire about you? What is your process?* The people who I am designed to minister to and impact cannot be reached by anyone else, so I have to carefully harness and use whatever has been deposited in me and blossom wherever I have been planted. As you walk into your

healing process, allow this to be your primary goal, believe in yourself, and the transformation only you can offer to yourself and the world. This is a way of life for me as I aspire to do whatever I believe the Lord has called me to.

7. **Take action** – I asked the Lord what He would have me to do. So, He has allowed me to go through this thing, He has kept me through it and matured me in His love to what end? It was by no means easy for me the first time I was asked to stand in front of a crowd and tell them all the horrible things I had endured. Some of it was embarrassing, and, in addition, I was very mindful that I had a family to protect. I had no intention for my now teenage children to learn certain aspects of my past, as I didn't want to tarnish the image of me they had in their minds. However, I soon realized that my pride and reputation were secondary to God's glory. My husband and I had to discuss everything with my children and help them understand that it was now my ministry and I must fulfill the call of God on my life. It's amazing how things can work out when we make a conscious decision to put God first in everything, so my family now supports my ministry fully. Embracing your divine destiny is the most important thing you can do. In this, healing takes place, forgiveness is birthed, and love returns in places where you were once hardened and hateful. You will once again become free and alive, and you will be able to

find joy; a joy that surpasses all understanding, not just for yourself but for others. As you embrace this call, some challenges will come your way, but always remember that you are loved and chosen by God for such a time as this.

8. **Take one step of faith** – I had no clue how to begin; I somehow knew I needed to, so I told God that whatever He said, I would do, not fully understanding what I was saying. Nevertheless, He knew my deepest thoughts and secrets. I remember when the Lord asked if I was sure I was ready to make the sacrifice, and it took several years to give Him a sincere yes. I struggled with the thought of forgoing all I knew, as I was afraid of what it would require of me, especially since I had struggled so much as a child and had worked so hard to have what I had and be where I was in the natural. I wasn't willing to risk putting it on the line for God and exercising reckless faith, but I have found so much joy since I surrendered everything, and now I use every opportunity to just do His work.

So, whether you have been raped, molested, physically abused, or neglected, whether you suffered from addiction or dealt with any other issue; it is possible for God to completely transform you into a beacon of hope for someone. Now is the time to decide in your heart that you have been in this unprofitable state for way too long. Now is the time to assess yourself and decide that enough is enough. In most cases, the people who have hurt us have moved on and are enjoying their lives with no memory or care of what transpired. We are the ones hurting, the ones who are constantly living in the cycle of rejection and ill choices that not only affect our physical, mental and spiritual health but that of our families as well. So, ask the Father to give you the ability to rise above the pain just enough to see His hands reaching out toward you with healing in His wings, ready to change your life and take you to new heights in Him.

CHAPTER 9

MY GLORY MOMENT

The word glory signifies magnificence, peculiarity, and importance. It is what we were created to be, and it is the unique grace and favor placed on us by God. Just like Joseph who was selected of all his brothers to become governor of Egypt, there is a glory moment for everyone willing to answer the call of God to walk a road that most dread or refuse to choose. No one is without a story, so there is always an opportunity for each of us to experience that moment of glory in our lifetime. We were all created with a divine blueprint for our lives that will align us with a certain work in our generation once we submit our lives and wills to God. We were not created to simply exist on this earth until we expire, but to live intentionally and purposefully to the glory of God the Father. Having come into the fullness of this knowledge I could not afford to be anything less than what was required to catapult me into my glory. I refused to go into my grave with buried talents and gifts and lost opportunities. Joseph was thrown into the pit to be buried by his own brothers who should have loved him and protected him, yet he was determined to protect his own vision that God gave him, the vision that those around him could not comprehend. He was imprisoned to be discouraged and frustrated, but even in the prison, his calling and purpose were strikingly evident. It has been said so many times and by so many people that the road to success is not an easy one; it includes being knocked over, disappointed, and distracted several times but having to get back up, brush off, and get back on track.

I was constantly reminded by those around me, including lecturers from the university I attended, family, and society, that I would never amount to anything. While everyone, at some point in their lives, will encounter discouragement or failure, I have learned our response to such encounters and the lessons we learn from them is most important. It is sometimes very difficult to conceptualize that God could use someone like me after all I have done and been. I believed my success was going back to school and earning a degree or two and be able to return to my community and prove to everyone I had defied the odds. I believed success meant owning a house on the hill, driving a nice car and living the dream, but I quickly understood that though those were major accomplishments, success was not defined by material acquisition but by a completely surrendered life to walk in purpose. I have never felt more fulfilled than I do today, and I know this is just the beginning of great things. I knew there was a call on my life but initially never understood exactly what it was. I was told by many men and women of God that God wanted to *"use me,"* and somewhere deep down I wanted to be used by God as well. After a while, I began searching for my gifting and seeking God about my calling, thinking it was time to launch out into the deep. I started listening to a certain woman of God and following her ministry closely, hoping I would learn from her experience, and I did. I learned that for her to be at the place in God where she was, she had gone through a host of setbacks and disappointments. I also remember when I asked the Lord to give me that anointing. I reflected on how Elisha followed Elijah in pursuit of the anointing that was on him, and God granted his request. It was with this same mindset I went to God seeking a similar anointing like this powerful woman of God, but God had already selected me for my purpose, not hers.

For several years, I believe God was challenging me to surrender as though I was walking closely with Him and doing all I thought was right. I was never truly at a place of total surrender, and that was where God wanted me to be for Him to do what He wanted to do. I was now working in ministry at my local church and doing well at whatever I was given to do, yet I refused to allow God to have complete control of my destiny. I knew I was afraid, because every time the Lord asked if I was ready for the anointing, if I was willing to pay the price, I refused to answer. I wasn't willing to even think about what that cost could be. Could it be my own dreams, children, husband, and career? I was not ready or willing to sacrifice any of the above, and, as a result, I never answered God. Time after time, that still small voice would come asking whether I was willing to pay the price, and each time I refused to respond.

The service was awesome, and the presence of God was truly in the midst that Sunday morning. The guest minister had just finished ministering and was seated at the back of the church when I went over to her to pray and thank her for coming. As I extended my hand to greet her and offer her a small thank you token, she held firmly to my hand with her head still bowed and asked me the question I had been evading for years. I stood there with an awestruck look on my face, close to tears, as I felt God had finally caught up with me, and there was no escape. She raised her head slowly, looked me dead in the eyes, and asked a second time, *"Are you ready to pay the price for the anointing?"* I said yes, but did I really mean it? I didn't think so, as immediately the thought of losing everything I had ever worked for raced through my mind. I walked away feeling dejected and helpless, as if I had no choice. I went home that evening, stood before my mirror, and really tried hard to find the yes or no to the pending question. I never told my husband about what happened because I was just too afraid of what I believe his response would be. I cried hard, contemplating my next move and the two options that were set before me, accept the call and pay the price, or reject it and still pay a price. Despite that clear, overwhelming encounter, I never said yes to God with my heart. I know my lips moved to the sound of a yes, but it was never genuine, as I was crippled with fear of what it would mean. As the months passed, I continued to operate in ministry without any concern for moving to the next level in God. I was content with my idea of effectiveness and was willing to forfeit everything He wanted to do through me. I failed to understand that I was robbing myself of the privilege and others of the opportunity to be transformed. It was not until later that same year when my husband and I were invited to minister to a group of young people at a prominent university that I really decided to say yes to God, no matter what it would cost me. I felt as if God laughed in my face when I finally did because after I decided to give up on everything and put all I knew on the line, I was given the assurance that He had no intention to rob me of my family or anything else I was worried about.

> *For I know the thoughts that I think toward you, says the LORD, thoughts of peace and not of evil, to give you a future and a hope. (Jeremiah 29:11).*

Sometimes all God wants is for us to see and acknowledge our own heart condition, to position us at the place to be used by Him. That night, I said yes to God once and for all, and it felt so good. Thank God for Shekinah Glory, who asked me the question one last time that night, *"If I told you what I really need, would your spirit still say yes......?"* I left that night with a renewed desire to know God more and to do His will. I decided I would do what I knew He was calling me to do. I left that night with one question in my mind—HOW?

The journey from there was a very adventurous one. I experienced warfare on a whole new level, but unlike before, I was not afraid, I was certain I wasn't fighting alone, and I was determined to press even harder when opposition came. The Lord began to download ideas into my spirit as I sought Him in prayer and fasting, and soon doors began to open for me to operate in my call. All the Father requires from us is a complete yes. He doesn't ask us to do anything He will not equip us for. Though we may feel incompetent or inadequate, He has placed in us that which we need to carry out the mandate He has given us. Things began to move along quickly, and before I knew it, my ministry was birthed. God had turned my mess into a powerful message of hope and healing. He had created something new and beautiful out of a pile of hurt and shame, using it to reveal the healing power which is in Jesus Christ that is able to transform lives and mend broken hearts.

You may feel you have hit rock bottom, that there is no more use for you and God cannot salvage any valuable thing from your huge pile of mess, but I want to discredit that lie and call it out for what it is. The songwriter reminds us that there isn't a broken vessel that God cannot mend. Like Joseph, David, and the Apostle Paul, God can pick you up, remove the shame, place you firmly on a new path, and use you mightily to change the world as you know it. All He wants from you is a made-up mind, a willingness to serve, and an available vessel to use.

Let us pray:

> *Father in Heaven, I come to You in the name of Jesus Christ, the Saviour of this world. I come to You in the name of Jesus Christ, the one who I entrust my whole life to. I ask You to locate and destroy every alliance that is working together to interrupt my progress; I ask You to destroy by fire every satanic embargo that is assigned to*

interfere with my purpose. I come against every destiny stealer and every dream-polluting demon and command them to be roasted by the fire of the living God. I pray that my losses will be converted to wins and that everything the enemy intended for bad, You will turn it around for good on my behalf. Let every power that is contracted to see to my demise be overruled now in the name of Jesus. Let them fall by the way and die because every hurt will return double to my enemy, Satan, as You position me to inflict severe blows to the kingdom of darkness. Father, I submit myself to You and to the purpose You have for me before this universe was formed, and I ask that You will anoint and appoint me over the nations and people You will have me to minister to. Let my will be lost in Yours, oh, Lord, and may heaven be blessed through me, in Jesus' name. Amen.

CHAPTER 10

STORIES OF SURVIVORS

When we decide to share our personal journey with others, it can be restorative for the person or persons who are still struggling with the effects of trauma caused by abuse, and it can also help them know they are not alone in their struggle. Remember, many others have experienced and may still be experiencing the pain of childhood sexual *abuse,* and stories of *those* who have overcome are a critical means of support for them. As you read the following chapter filled with riveting truths from the lives of adult *survivors* of childhood trauma, I pray it will help to break down the barriers of loneliness and isolation, destroy the barricade of shame and self-hate, and give you hope and optimism that you too can be a source of strength to someone else. Most *survivors* will never see justice and will have to depend on the help of others like themselves to overcome the past and walk into the future.

SURVIVOR NUMBER 1

I grew up being very frustrated, bitter, angry, and revengeful most of the time, but no one seemed to understand the reasons for my behaviour. At the age of nine, I was fondled by a close family friend who I loved and respected. I did not mention it to anyone at the time, as I was afraid. A few years later, at the age of fifteen, I was sexually assaulted by my dad, who was also my role model and mentor. This took everything away from me, including my pride and happiness. Two days after my dad raped me, my brother raped me as well, and that tore the rest of me apart, leaving me in a lot of emotional and physical pain. This continued to happen over and over until I believed that it was normal. My mother was told about it eventually, but she didn't believe me, so I became even more bitter toward my family and hated my mother because I believed she didn't care about me. My father continued to rape me over and over until I became pregnant. He forced me to have an abortion and took me to one of his friends to have it done. I hated myself and wanted desperately to die. I felt I had no reason to go on, that my life wasn't worth living anymore. I entered a lesbian relationship at about age sixteen, as I was developing an intense, uncontrollable attraction to the same sex and a detestable passionate hatred for the opposite sex. I started smoking, drinking, and even masturbating, hoping it would help free me from the pain, but it didn't. I later became involved in prostitution and found pleasure in being in the street, thinking I could have sex with who I wanted; at least it would be my choice. I had no one to talk to, and I didn't trust anymore, so I continued to release my emotions through prostitution. I was gang-raped by three men while in the streets, and they threatened to kill me. But as I saw my life flash before my eyes, I begged them not to kill me, forgetting I previously had a desire to die.

A week later, my uncle raped me. I was at a desperate place because I didn't care anymore, as the people who I loved and trusted hurt me deeply and ruined my life. I was invited to church by a friend and I went hoping I would find some sort of escape. I thought I could find comfort going there for a while. While attending the church, I was raped by the pastor and became pregnant by him as well. Once again, I was forced to do another abortion. I thought that was the end; I felt like everything was caving in on me. I felt like I was a sex toy and so I was treated as one; life meant nothing. I felt rejected, down, and I felt like an outcast, wondering if my life would be better and asking myself what I had done wrong in my life. I felt I was good for nothing, worthless, and should be locked away from society. I finally tried committing suicide many times, but even that failed. I felt like I was going crazy, as it was just too much for me to bear.

In 2016, I was raped again; this time it was so bad I was hospitalized, and even the doctors thought I would not make it. Despite everything I have been through, I am still here today. God has restored me and has sent me several people to stand by me and help me along this path. They showed me how they have been through the same thing and how they have come out. I thank God for my mentor and motivator, who helped me to keep coping. Even when I felt all hope was lost, she has never given up on me. She helped me recognize that I didn't have to do all that I was doing and has helped me through the deliverance process. I am proud to say, with their help and with the help of Almighty God, I am delivered and don't do the things I used to do anymore.

SURVIVOR NUMBER 2

I was living with my mother and stepdad in the country. My mother would go to church every Thursday for a prayer meeting or something, leaving me in the care of my stepdad. He was always nice to me, except when he was drunk and cursed at us for no reason. One night, my mom left as usual for church, but that night something happened. My stepdad entered the room and asked me if I was okay. I said yes, and he said he only wanted to make sure. He sat on the edge of my bed and began to say I was a pretty girl, and he loved me, and I was nothing like my mother. He placed his hand on my belly and began to touch me in other places that made me feel uncomfortable. He did not have sex with me that night, but he told me it was a little secret between us and I should not tell my mom, as she would be mad at me if I did.

Every Thursday night when my mom went to church, he came into my room to ensure I was "okay" and reminded me at the end that my mom would be upset if she found out, so I never told her. One night, he said I was a big girl now, and he would show me how big girls love their daddy. He took off my underwear and had sex with me that night. It was so painful I thought I would die. When he was finished, he kissed me on my forehead and reminded me that my mom would be even more upset if she found out he loved me, so, of course, I never told. My stepdad had sex with me every week, and although I did not like it, I never said anything. Once my mother left for church, I anticipated what would happen next. By the time I was fourteen, I started to have sex with different boys at my school as well as those in my neighbourhood. My stepdad found out about it, and after giving me the worst beating of my life, he reported it to my mother, who beat me again. That Thursday, when my mother went to church, he came into my room as usual and said that since I was a big woman, he would show me how big woman did things. He had sex with me violently in several different orifices while slapping me and calling me names. I knew my mother would be upset if I told, so I ran away from home the following night. I had nowhere to go, so I walked around until it was dark. Since I hadn't eaten that day, I became sick and began to cry as I walked along the street. Someone saw me and asked what was wrong, and I told him what happened. He said he would get me something to eat, so I went with him. He asked me where I was going to stay and offered to put me up for the night. While I was getting settled for bed, he told me I needed to do a favour for him, to which I agreed. That night, he and his friend had sex with me. I began to desire more sex and ended up having sex with men for money. I was seventeen by now and had met an older girl who said she would teach me the "work." I stayed with her for a while, and we made lots of money working in the streets. I became uncomfortable in my situation because my Christian background contrasted with this way of life. I began attending a church nearby and later gave my life to Jesus. I find comfort now in the fact that He will take care of me. I regret not forgiving my stepdad before he died, but I believe God has healed me from the hurt, so I released him from my heart even though I won't get a chance to tell him.

SURVIVOR NUMBER 3

I was eleven years old when it first started. I was home alone, my mother was living and working overseas, and my father, with whom I lived, was probably at the bar getting his fill. The neighbour, a near-sixty-year-old man, came up to me like a pouncing wolf, grabbed me, and began rubbing himself against me until he was satisfied. After he released me, shock took over my body, and I went numb with fear. I felt I could tell no one, so I kept it to myself.

The story of my uninvited ordeals never stopped there, as my dad was old and incapable of caring for me, so my mom rented a home for my young brother, who was now in the picture, and me. We had a caregiver on the weekends who assisted with the household chores but, for the most part, I had to run the home; cooking, cleaning, and taking care of a child. Family members would also chip in from time to time and stay with me. One such family member only added more mental strain and more physical damage. Not only was I having to physically take care of my home, but I would end up working for him too, and he would make it known when he was not satisfied. He would get very angry sometimes, hitting me forcefully and often expressing his sexual interest in me.

I was playing with my brother once, and as I stood on the bed, he entered the room, laid across the bed, and began to stare at me. He then stretched up toward me as if to play. I said, *"Be careful of letting me fall."* He replied, *"That's what I want you to do—fall on me,"* pointing to and grabbing his crotch to ensure I knew what he meant. I felt disgusted but said nothing because I feared his blind wrath. Not having anyone to tell gave me a feeling of abandonment that was all too familiar. He continued to make advances, until one day when I was visiting my grandmother, and I was sent to go with him to tend to our family livestock, he began to draw closer and closer as we walked along the lonely road, trotting deeper and deeper into the woods. He grabbed me and pulled me toward him, bringing both of us toward a big boulder on the side of the road, where he had sex with me. I thought I would end up dead that day because I knew the anger within him. I was only fourteen years old at the time, and he warned me not to tell, knowing I feared him. We left the bushes and went back home. I was shaken to the core but told no one about what happened. I did not feel I had a close enough relationship with my grandmother to say anything, and everyone else was emotionally and physically distant. Having to deal with this mess, I began searching for the best mediums to let it out. I tried church, and it worked for a while, but soon the façade ate away at me. I was failing at school because I never knew how to cope. At one point I remember calling my mother in tears and telling her I cannot sit my final exams; which was a critical school leaving exam. I was forced to go, with tears streaming down my face. I accomplished nothing on the test. My life went down a slippery slope throughout high school and even more so after. Feeling like I had no value or self-worth, I threw myself into a reckless relationship, drugs, and parties. It didn't matter anymore, as I knew no real love. It was not until I truly met Jesus as an adult that I could share how I had struggled and be delivered from the pain and hatred that was fixed in my heart for my entire family. Through the Love of Jesus Christ, my Lord, I was able to let go of the pain and truly love and forgive those who had hurt me for so many years.

These three sisters were forced to walk a path that wasn't easy, but one thing they all can attest to is that despite all they had been through, Jesus has brought peace and comfort to them in a way that nothing else could. I encourage you to surrender the hurts to Jesus. He alone is able to heal you completely and set you on the path to recovery.

CHAPTER 11

WHAT THE NUMBERS ARE SAYING

This chapter is intended to demonstrate the degree and prevalence of child sexual abuse in Jamaica and the Caribbean, providing a glimpse of what is happening in the world. It has already been evident that this issue is rarely discussed, even in our own culture, and is very difficult to control or bring to an end. As I read different research papers and scholarly articles written by various individuals, I found that it is not only taboo in Jamaica but also in many other nations and cultures across the globe. During my research, the prevalence of child sexual abuse was found to be alarmingly high mostly in India and some places in Africa, and it was not readily talked about due to the risks of being excommunicated from families and communities as well as the shame brought to the woman or girl being, or has been, abused. Nevertheless, even though the numbers in these underdeveloped countries seem to be extremely high, the prevalence of child sexual abuse is still at an unacceptably high rate throughout the world. This is obviously a huge problem that still affects many of our children every day. One of the main reasons that contribute to the poor control of such an issue is that the cases reported by the authorities usually do not represent the total number of victims because many cases, such as my own and those mentioned in this book, never got reported to them at all in the first place.

Studies have revealed that one in every five females and one in every ten males have been sexually abused globally every year and that sixty percent (60%) of these incidences occur before age twelve.

Another source states that "While most abuse is hidden and up-to-date *statistics* are scarce, it is known that nearly 150 million girls and 73 million boys under 18 around the world have experienced forced sexual intercourse or other forms of *sexual violence* worldwide."[1]

It has also been demonstrated that in approximately 95% of these cases, the abuser is a family member, close family friend, neighbour, or someone trusted by the family, which tends to be consistent with what I have seen and heard.

A study recently conducted by the Georgia State University in the United States shows that child sexual abuse in the US costs up to 1.5 million dollars per child death.

The burden on the economy related to child sexual abuse is enormous and, if remedied, can and will positively impact not only the victims and their families but the nation as a whole. Despite this finding, the potential of eradicating this disease is far-reaching due to underreporting as well as other potential issues.

As we take a closer look at the numbers in the Caribbean region, we will also see that we are not invulnerable to this epidemic and that many of our children tend to undergo severe trauma during and after sexual abuse. Poverty, crime, and drugs are just some of the challenges facing small Caribbean nations, and these predispose young children and teenagers to abuse, including sexual abuse. Poverty travels

---

[1]   https://www.unicef.org/infobycountry/jamaica_62479.html

hand in hand with high levels of unemployment, especially for younger folks, and prevents some people from being able to acquire the necessary skills to earn a living in their economies, which leaves young people to have children with no means to properly care for them, hence placing them at risk to be victimized.

With such soaring levels of unemployment and escalating lack of economic sustenance in some Caribbean communities, we tend to be bombarded with drug and human trafficking. This is a fertile soil for criminal and gang activity to be increased across nations and has been the case for decades now. You may be aware of a stomach-turning video recently circulating of a small child performing fellatio on an adult in one of the Caribbean countries or the various recent reports of church leaders in Jamaica being found guilty of these perverted acts that cause extensive damage to young lives. These are just a few of the many cases, some of which we never hear about. Despite advances in educating the population and the region as a whole about the importance of reporting incidences of childhood sexual abuse, many still refuse to come forward, and several stories remain untold.

It is, therefore, our responsibility to play our part in ensuring that these children are protected and that the full extent of the law is meted out to those who inflict these deep-seated internal and sometimes external wounds on our children by becoming vocal on the topic and doing everything we can to advocate for the victims, follow up with court cases, and bring awareness to the people. We must bring back to life the approach of a village raising every child.

The United Nations Children's Fund (UNICEF), an agency formed by the United Nations General Assembly in 1946, was initially concerned with improving the health and nutrition of children and mothers throughout the world but has now extended its reach to other issues and is continuously working to improve the lives of children and families in the Caribbean for over seventy years. They have worked with the United Nations and other United Nations Agencies to make sure that children are on the global schema and strike a balance between systematic research and realistic solutions for children.

According to a document provided by this agency, it is said that 42.8% of females younger than twelve years old have been sexually abused, generally in places where they should be protected. This takes place across all societal and economical planes and age groups and occurs in homes, schools, other institutions such as churches, or even on a community level. It states that the abuse often begins when the child is less than ten years old and continues throughout a child's adolescent life and that children with disabilities are at a greater risk of experiencing higher levels of sexual abuse than children from the general populace. It was also noted that of all the Caribbean countries, only six have a specific policy in place to protect children from violent behaviour and of such programs, it is said that they have insufficient human and financial resources to alleviate the growing problem of child sexual abuse; they lack public awareness on the issue of child sexual abuse; and they do not rely on adequate data collection system.

Despite this shortfall, there are several mechanisms put in place to help prevent the occurrences of child sexual abuse. These are known as the National Protocol for the Prevention of Child Abuse and refer to protocols and guidelines for reporting, including twenty-four-hour hotlines for reporting child sexual abuse, shelters or places of safety for children, and an obligation to report child sexual abuse, not only if one is aware, but if it is suspected to have happened or will happen in the future.

These are the same protocols that have been in place in Jamaica as of 2004 after the inception of the Child Care and Protection Act. Yet, whenever an alarm is sounded about an abuse incident in our communities, we tend to become very vocal about it as if it is ludicrous while the victims continue to suffer. It is sad that even in modern times such as these in Jamaica, there still is a mentality that anyone who reports such occurrences should pay with their lives because they are seen as informers; as a result, many individuals will be afraid to come forward, even if they are not in agreement with the perpetrators or if they are victims themselves. This was the case in my situation, as I was beaten by one of my abusive family members when I spoke up about the abuse eight years later.

Notwithstanding, the government has been doing an extensive amount of groundwork as it relates to bringing the issue to the table, and campaigns such as "Focusing on Sexual Abuse in Children," which took place in 2012, spearheaded by the Department of Justice, in collaboration with the OCR, UNICEF, CDA, and CISOCA, is one of the many that has helped bring awareness to the matter and have seen more persons joining forces to let their voices be heard. In light of this positive response, I believe the Minister of Justice at the time was able to assert that the increase in numbers from a little over 460 reported cases in 2007 to more than 6,000 reported cases in 2009 may suggest a positive response to being sensitized about one's civic responsibility and knowledge of how to make such a report than it is an increase in the actual incidence. So, some headway has been made in the effort to speak up about the issue from a national as well as a communal level.

The University of the West Indies in Trinidad and Tobago also developed the "Teddy Bear Campaign," using the image of a teddy bear with a band-aid over its heart and the tagline "Break the Silence." This initiative has mobilized a wide range of government and non-governmental partners to protect children from sexual abuse.[2]

In addition, the Office of the Children's Registry (OCR) has reported that more than 13,000 cases of child abuse were recorded for the period January to December 2015. This

---

[2]   https://www.dominicavibes.dm/news-58225/

represents 18 out of every 1000 children in the country for that period and an 18.7% increase over the previous year. It was also established that more than 9,000 cases were being reported for the first time.

Over an eight-year period, from 2007 to 2015, the Office of Children Registry recorded greater than 16,790 reports of sexual abuse against children (see table below).

Years	Males	Females	Unknown
2007	12	106	3
2008	74	1085	12
2009	125	1577	6
2010	99	1470	5
2011	119	2551	1
2012	205	2542	9
2013	258	3118	10
2014	377	3008	18
2015	380	3419	12
Total	1649	18876	71
		Grand Total	20,596

Table derived from information provided by the OCR website.

As we move forward, I desire to see every child who is abused vindicated and receive the necessary help to take hold of their lives and be able to live purposefully. That is one reason I believe God mandated me to write about my experience. Child sexual abuse is not the problem of the victim or the family;

it is a national and universal crisis that, if not addressed, will see a society failing as the future generation continues to be crippled by the effects of this endemic. I share my story to stimulate your minds to believe you can overcome the odds and change your own life and others and to empower you to live intentionally and to accomplish the great things God has in store for you.

EPILOGUE

WHAT'S NEXT?

It is with great pleasure that I write to you at this point, as now we have come to the end of this journey and the beginning of an awesome new one filled with new possibilities and expectations. I imagine it has been a long and difficult, sometimes even painful process of acknowledging and confronting the hurt and the shame. It has required much effort and determination to forgive and release those who have hurt you, but you made it, and I am so proud of you. You are now renewed, restored, and ready to be used by God, a vessel of honor, sanctified and useful to the master. Give yourself a tap on the shoulder and let's roll!

Now that you have been set free, there is so much to do, and no time to waste. First, grab your journal and begin to write down all you would like to accomplish over the next few weeks and months. Ensure that the goals you set are realistic and prepare to move at your own pace according to what God is doing. This is not about someone else's expectations of you, but about finding yourself and identifying what the Lord wants you to do with your experiences and the lessons learned.

One of the most challenging things is trusting again and allowing people inside your inner sanctum, so spend quality time seeking the Lord about when to let people in and who is good for you. Most importantly, live and breathe and not worry about what you will do next. God has a way to align everything as long as we depend on Him to do it. It is always good to find a mentor who can help you along, especially in the first stage of your new life. There will be challenges internally and externally and having a good support system will be crucial in how you move forward. This person can also serve as an accountability partner who will keep a consistent inventory on you achieving your personal and God-assigned goals.

After I allowed God to heal me and realized I had a different option than remaining in the mess I was in, it wasn't always easy to just walk out boldly into that new path. There were many times when I was scared of what the future held and what it meant to leave my *'normal'* behind. One thing I know for sure is that I would not have been able to do it alone, and that's why it is important to identify spiritual people who can help and encourage you along the way. There were also some practical things I needed to do to refine and sustain the change that had been made in me, and those were some of the most difficult but necessary decisions that were instrumental in my current position.

I had to change my perspective – After the abuse began, my whole view on life, people, and God changed. I never knew God for who He was, but my idea of Him was that He was loving and caring. That changed drastically, and I began to see Him as uncaring and selfish. I had to retrain my thoughts and attitudes toward Him to understand and accept that He is perfect in all His ways and never does anything to harm His children, even when they do not acknowledge Him for who He is. I had to learn that the blueprint He had for my life was a uniquely designed one, which would challenge me to grow to new heights and deeper depths. I had to understand that He is sovereign and has ultimate control over all things and sometimes will allow not-so-nice things to happen to bring about life-changing results. I had to learn the most important truth of all time—that He loved me.

The people in my circle, at the time, in my opinion, were all bad. I felt there was little or no good in anyone, and I entered every relationship, whether casual or otherwise, with the mindset to hope for the best but to expect the worst. That was a coping mechanism that would prevent me from being hurt again, so no one could really get into my personal space except superficially. I decided I would get what I wanted first, just in case the person proved to be a failure like everyone else had done. I had to learn to obey the commandments of my Father to love my neighbour as myself. I had to change that thought pattern and learn to love my mother, my grandmother, and my abusive family members, even though they had hurt me deeply and I didn't feel they deserved to be loved. I had to learn to allow people to be who they are and try to see the good in them instead of the bad and to treat them accordingly.

I had to accept that life does not always produce happy moments and that, like an echocardiograph, if there are no ups and downs, it simply means we are dead. I had to embrace and celebrate the positives and accept and learn from the negatives. I had to use them as motivation to do better next time and recognize every failure as one closer attempt at success.

I had to change my attitude – I became angry, cold, and selfish in my pursuit to protect myself from the elements of life. It was easy for me to physically and even verbally attack anyone who seemed to be a threat to my safety and, as a result, ended up in many violent situations, one of which led me to the police station and almost resulted in me getting arrested. I saw people as targets and preys and believed they saw me the same way, so I always had my defense intact and was ready for the war by any means necessary.

My heart was like an iceberg, and I had lost any knowledge of how to truly love others from a place of sincerity. I carefully selected the songs I listened to and the movies I watched, as these ministered to the hurt and the pain and made me feel entitled to my behavior. I had to gradually let go of my appetite for these sources of false comfort and instead learn to find comfort in the Word of God, which eventually taught me how to relate to people around me, even though I still have a way to go. I thank God for those He placed in my life that helped me find hope and healing in my faith.

I had always lived on my own, made my own decisions, and answered to no one. I told myself from a tender age that no one would ever again make decisions on my behalf. I was self-sufficient, independent, and proud. I cared zero for other people's opinions of me and was only concerned about getting things done my way or no way. That was obviously not a fertile ground on which to develop lasting relationships; it only worked in superficial situations where others' feelings did not matter. As a child of God, with a new mindset, I had to learn to co-exist with others and value their opinions and feelings, sometimes putting my own aside to ensure others were treated well. I remember crying out to God and asking why He had turned me into such a softie because I now had feelings and had to come face to face with them. Today, I dedicate my whole life to helping others, and I know that had it not been for the love and grace of Jesus Christ, that would not be possible.

I had to change my friends – Many, if not all, of my friends were doing drugs, drinking, partying, and sleeping around. I had no one in my circle of friends who I believe was ever sober for more than a few hours. So, to develop and maintain a serious relationship with God, I realized I had to disassociate myself from these influences and seek new friends. That was a very difficult, and often lonely process because I still had issues with trusting people and determining who to allow in. I was attending church now, but I had a reputation, and many church folks wanted nothing to do with a sinner like me, as their pearly whiteboard of a life would be tainted by associating themselves with my type. I finally became friends with a couple who were leaders in the church and began to trust them with my struggles. I then found that my life story and challenges were the hot topics in every youth meeting or informal gathering. Church hurt is one of the most painful and destructive things anyone can ever experience, and if you have ever been hurt by church people, you will understand what I mean. Despite the hurt and shame I experienced, I decided that I was not going back to the place of normalcy, so I pursued other relationships that eventually proved to be emotionally and spiritually healthy.

I also had to change my contact information, such as my phone number and email address, to radically eliminate some people from my life. One person threatened me with violence when she discovered that what we had ended and there was no chance of any reconnection, but I wasn't afraid of her threats; I was more concerned about my own growth by now.

As you enter a new season of your life, you will experience some highs and some lows, you will have victories as well as challenges, and there will be days when you feel nothing at all. It is important to remain consistent in your efforts to connect with God. Even when the season is cold and seemingly lifeless, do not retreat to where you are coming from but understand that it takes four seasons to make a beautiful year, and all of them are not bright and sunny.

Today, I accept that I am still under construction, and many days I fail to be the best me, but I know that I want to change lives and positively effect change in those around me. So even when I fail to measure up one day, I take a bold leap of faith into the next morning with an increased desire to make that day count for something.

FROM MY HEART TO YOURS

You are just one person and may not be able to impact the masses with the little resources you have. I understand that you may ask yourself what you can do to change anything. You may still be hurting or crippled with fear of the unknown, or you may not even have finished school or have a great job, but you can make a difference in one life, even if that one life is your own. For too long, we have reclined in our places of comfort or discomfort, watching life pass us by, knowing full well that this is not all there is to it, but doing nothing because we either do not want to get involved or simply are afraid to take that one step of faith and let our voices be heard. I challenge you today to open yourself up and talk to someone you know who is affected by the disease of childhood sexual abuse, so they can get the help they need. If you are still at a place of hurt but want to move from it, reach out to someone who can help you; a pastor, a teacher, or counselor, and take back your life, making every effort to live it purposefully.

Your life will never be the same when the barriers to living are broken down. Allow God to heal you and watch how far and wide your reach will become.

REFERENCES

Finkelhor, D. (2008, March 31). "Child Sexual Abuse Statistics." The National Centre for Victims of Crimes. http://victimsofcrime.org/media/reporting-on-child-sexual-abuse/child-sexual-abuse-statistics

Hahn, T. (2012, May 18). "Fighting child sexual abuse in the Caribbean." UNICEF. https://www.unicef.org/health/jamaica_62479.html

Singh, M.M, Parsekar, S.S, Nair, S.N. (2014 Oct-Dec). "An Epidemiological Overview of Child Sexual Abuse." J Family Med Prim Care. https://www.ncbi.nlm.nih.gov/pmc/articles/PMC4311357/

Unknown. (2014, April 10). "Sexual Abuse Against Girls and Boys in the Caribbean." UNICEF. https://www.unicef.org/easterncaribbean/ECAO__Sexual_Abuse.pdf

Made in the USA
Middletown, DE
07 September 2019